YOU CAN TEACH

MANDOLIN

by Dix Bruce

Here's what's included:

- Nineteen easy songs
- Tuning the mandolin
- Nineteen mandolin solos
- All common mandolin chords
- Mandolin accompaniment strums
- Basic pick technique, tremolo, and double stops

- Handy scale, chord, and transposition chart
- "Sources" section for further study
- Elementary note and music reading
- Scales, keys, and transposition
- Beginning music theory
- Chord appendix

CD Contents

1. Introduction (1:02)
2. Tuning (2:19)
3. He's Got The Whole World-Slow/Page 16-17 (1:37)
4. He's Got The Whole World-Faster (:51)
5. First Strum (:33)
6. Hush Little Baby-Intro. (:51)
7. Hush Little Baby-Slow/Page 18-19 (1:06)
8. Hush Little Baby-Faster (:54)
9. Streets of Laredo-Intro. (:37)
10. Streets of Laredo-Slow/Page 20-21 (1:30)
11. Streets of Laredo-Regular (:43)
12. Kumbaya-Intro./Page 22 (:51)
13. Kumbaya-Slow/Page 23 (1:04)
14. Kumbaya-Regular (:48)
15. John B. Sails-Intro. (1:04)
16. John B. Sails-Slow/Page 25-27 (1:00)
17. John B. Sails-Regular (:55)
18. I Ride an Old Paint-Intro. (1:05)
19. I Ride an Old Paint-Slow/Page 30 (1:09)
20. I Ride an Old Paint-Regular (:57)
21. Careless Love-Intro. (1:01)
22. Careless Love-Slow/Page 33 (1:18)
23. Careless Love-Regular (:48)

24. Sportin' Life-Intro. (2:51)
25. Sportin' Life-Slow/Page 38-39 (1:03)
26. Sportin' Life-Variation (:45)
27. Sportin' Life-Regular (:46)
28. Fair Tender Ladies-Slow/Page 40-41 (1:05)
29. Fair Tender Ladies-Regular (1:31)
30. The Cuckoo-Intro. (:36)
31. The Cuckoo-Slow/Page 44-45 (:54)
32. The Cuckoo-Faster (1:16)
33. The Cruel War-Intro. (1:59)
34. The Cruel War-Slow/Page 48-49 (1:00)
35. The Cruel War-Faster (:49)
36. Nine Pound Hammer-Intro. (1:27)
37. Nine Pound Hammer-Slow/Page 51 (:56)
38. Nine Pound Hammer-Reg. (1:12)
39. The Bluegrass Chop Chord (:53)
40. Take a Drink on Me-Slow/Page 54 (:55)
41. Take a Drink on Me-Regular (:41)
42. Transposing (2:03)
43. Notes (1:24)
44. Notes (:39)
45. Stringin'-Slow/Page 64 (:35)
46. Stringin'-Regular (:45)
47. Scales-Major/Page 67 (2:32)

48. Scales-Flat Keys (1:53)
49. Eighth Notes, Pick Directions, Examples (:59)
50. More Examples (:21)
51. No Name Rag-Slow/Page 74 (1:00)
52. No Name Rag-Regular (1:17)
53. No Name Rag-Transposition (:59)
54. No Name Rag-Key of D (:48)
55. Dotted Notes (1:38)
56. Swing Low, Sweet Chariot-Slow/Page 77 (:55)
57. Swing Low, Sweet Chariot-Regular (1:10)
58. Hammer Ons, Pulls & Slides (1:23)
59. Sally Goodin-Slow/Page 79 (:48)
60. Sally Goodin-Regular (1:06)
61. Sally Goodin-With Slides (:43)
62. Tremolo (:29)
63. Fair & Tender Ladies-Slow/Page 82 (:52)
64. Fair & Tender Ladies-Regular (:44)
65. All Through the Night-Excerpt/Page 84 (:32)
66. All Through the Night-Slow/Page 86 (1:24)
67. All Through the Night-Regular (1:04)
68. So Long Ending (:31)

This book is available either by itself or packaged with a companion audio and/or video recording. If you have purchased the book only, you may wish to purchase the recordings separately. The publisher strongly recommends using a recording along with the text to assure accuracy of interpretation and make learning easier and more enjoyable.

3 4 5 6 7 8 9 0

Visit us on the Web at www.melbay.com — E-mail us at email@melbay.com

Contents

Dix Bruce is a writer and award-winning musician from the San Francisco Bay Area. He edited **Mandolin World News** from 1978 to 1984 and has recorded two albums with bluegrass mandolin legend Frank Wakefield. He recently completed a solo folk recording, *My Folk Heart,* and has just released a band recording of string swing & jazz, *Tuxedo Blues,* with many of his original compositions. He is a columnist for the Fretted Instrument Guild of America newsletter, was a frequent contributor to **FRETS** magazine, and writes for **Acoustic Guitar**. He has taught mandolin, guitar, and bass for nearly twenty years. He also tours and records with The Royal Society Jazz Orchestra, a big band from San Francisco.

This book is dedicated to David Grisman for his patience, generosity, and, above all, his music. Thanks for tirelessly suffering endless questions, graciously sharing time, information, know-how, books, tapes and records. Thanks for showing how good things can sound and how much fun music can be.

Special thanks to Becky Smith, Tom Beckeny, Jack Tuttle, Annie Johnston, Ken Eidson, and Liz Lamson for their help in producing this book and to Kathi Bruce for her excellent editorial suggestions.

Also by Dix Bruce:

BackUp Trax – a series of play-along book & tape sets. Learn melodies and practice soloing and improvising by playing along with great rhythm sections. Each melody from the book is recorded at slow speed (with just guitar accompaniment) and regular speed (with whole band), then the band plays several choruses of the tune while you supply the melody or solo! Stereo cassette tapes allow you to isolate recorded melodies from rhythm section for study. Repeat a song, at either speed, as many times as you wish, perfecting phrases, melodies and solos in a band context — they'll jam all night long! Beginners can practice basic skills while more advanced players can hone their improvisational chops — each at their own individual learning rates. You'll be amazed at your progress. Here's what's currently available:

BackUp Trax: Old Time & Fiddle Tunes Vol. 1 (Mel Bay). Learn melodies and practice soloing on fourteen of the most popular old time & fiddle tunes: *Temperance Reel, Sally Goodin, Blackberry Blossom, Over the Waves, Beaumont Rag, Red Haired Boy, June Apple, Salty Dog, The Wayfaring Stranger, Black Mountain Rag, Arkansas Traveller, Soldier's Joy, Billy in the Lowground* and *Old Joe Clark*. Available in two editions: Fiddle/Mandolin with mandolin tablature and Guitar/Banjo with guitar and banjo tablature.

BackUp Trax: Swing & Jazz Vol. 1 (Mel Bay). Great string rhythm section: guitar, mandolin, and bass, new acoustic music-style. Learn solos and practice melodies and improvisation on twelve of the most played standard progressions in swing & jazz: cycle of fifths, major & minor blues, two-five-one changes, one-six-two-five changes, and much more. Four editions: one for guitar, mandolin, violin and other C instruments (includes mandolin and guitar tablature), B♭ for clarinet and most saxes, E♭ for alto sax, and Bass for trombone, bass, etc.

BackUp Trax: Traditional Jazz & Dixieland Vol. 1 (Mel Bay). Play-along book & tape set featuring trad jazz rhythm section — banjo/guitar, tuba/bass, piano & drums with trumpet leads. Learn melodies and practice improvising on the most popular trad jazz and Dixieland tunes (*Saints, Down by the Riverside, Bill Bailey, Make Me A Pallet on Your Floor, St. James Infirmary, Just a Closer Walk, St. Louis Blues, Frankie & Johnnie*, 16 in all).

Beginning Country Guitar Handbook/tape (Mel Bay) teaches all the basics of country guitar: chords, backup, bass runs, leads, bluegrass picking, introductory music theory, soloing & improvisation, how to use a capo, how to transpose, and much more. Includes eighteen great traditional American folk/country songs with lyrics. Stereo tape has all book songs and examples at slow and regular speeds.

For information write: Dix Bruce, c/o Musix, PO Box 231005, Pleasant Hill, CA 94523.

Beginning at the Beginning

It's a great little instrument, the mandolin. Tuned like a fiddle with frets like a guitar, it can play classical, bluegrass, jazz, rock, country, folk, or any music the player's heart desires. It can sound soft and sweet or loud and funky, laid-back bluesy or jumping and jivey. It's not difficult to learn and can be the most fun you'll ever have without laughing.

As a mandolin player, you'll amaze your friends, be the life of every party, and do your parents proud. You'll be in the swift company of greats like Jethro Burns, David Grisman, Bill Monroe, Tiny Moore, Ricky Skaggs, Keith Harris, and others.

You Can Teach Yourself Mandolin is primarily a "teach-yourself" text with "play-along" examples and tunes demonstrated on tape. It is aimed at helping you get started immediately on your own road to mandolinhood by giving you an overview of the basics of the mandolin and mandolin playing. You'll learn about the instrument and its parts, how to tune, how to play common chords and useful strums, how to accompany yourself and others on a repertoire of popular folk songs, and how to read simple melodies. From this basic foundation you can go on to further study in whatever mandolin style interests you.

This book is divided into two sections, "Part I – Chords" and "Part II – Basic Note Reading." Everything in the book can be heard on the stereo cassette tape, from the first tuning tones and chord strums to the more advanced song melodies. Many of the taped examples are presented at both regular and half speed to allow you the best chance of understanding the concepts discussed and demonstrated. All musical examples are written in both standard music notation and tablature, a number-and-position-based notation system.

Whether you're new to music and an absolute beginner on the instrument, know a few chords and a strum or two, or can pick out a few melodies, it's a good idea to start at the beginning of the book. (You knew I'd say that, didn't you?) Before you jump in, skim through the book to familiarize yourself with the range of material covered, the types of songs included, and the helpful charts and lists included at the back of the book.

Read the text first, check out the music, and then listen to and play along with the tape. If you're in the advanced beginner category, concentrate on the things that are new and skip over those that you already know. The tape can speed your learning by letting you hear how all the strums, songs, and melodies from the text sound. Use it as a picking pal and get into the habit of playing along. It'll help you to adjust to playing with other people. If you're an absolute beginner, you may have trouble at first keeping up with the tape. If you find this happening, spend a little more time practicing on your own.

To make best use of the book/cassette format, zero the counter on your cassette player at the very beginning of each side. Then, as you listen to the tape the first time, write the counter numbers in the book beside each tune (e.g., "Streets of Laredo–A 206" or "E♭ scale–B 105" —letters denote tape sides). Individual sections of the tape will then be a snap to find and review. (We didn't include counter numbers in the tape package because the counters of individual cassette machines vary so greatly.)

Make a special effort to keep yourself involved both with listening and playing. (Check out the "Sources" section in the back of the book for listening suggestions.)

Most importantly, be patient with yourself. You can't learn to play mandolin overnight. If you come across something you're having difficulty with or a musical concept that you don't understand, take a break and come back to it. (Just be sure to come back to it!) After all, this is music . . . it's supposed to be **FUN!**

Though *You Can Teach Yourself Mandolin* self-teaches, it can't respond to your questions or correct your bad habits. Because of this, you may find it helpful, especially if you're new to music and the mandolin, to consult an experienced teacher from time to time for face-to-face instruction.

So, let's begin!

Dix Bruce

"Breakfast of Champions"   *Illustration copyright Deborah Cotter. Used by permission.*

The Mandolin & Its Parts

The diagrams below will familiarize you with the various parts of the mandolin as they are referred to in the text. Though mandolins come in several different sizes and shapes, most look something like the two styles shown below.

A-Style Mandolin   **F-Style Mandolin**

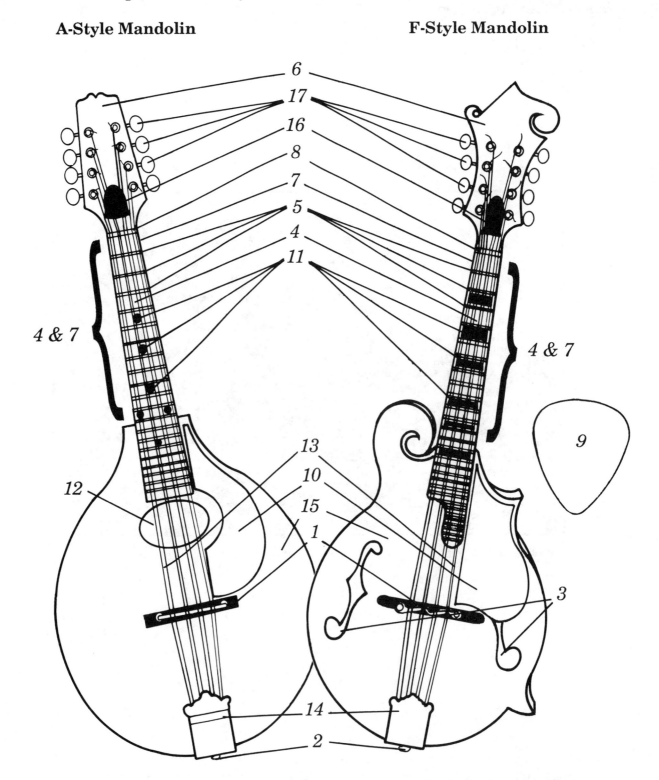

Bridge – 1

Strings rest on the bridge, which conducts their vibration to the resonant top of the mandolin. Nearly all mandolin bridges "float," held onto the top only by the tension of the strings. As such, bridges move and may need to be corrected periodically to insure proper intonation. Some bridges are height adjustable by two small wheels imbedded in the bridge itself.

Endpin – 2

The endpin holds one end of your strap. If you have an F-style mandolin, the other end of the strap goes around the curl. If your mandolin doesn't have a curl, tie the other end onto the headstock (6), under the strings near the nut (8).

F-Hole – 3

F-holes are shaped like a script letter *F* as on a violin. After the music goes round and round, it comes out here. Other mandolins, like the A-hole, have oval-shaped soundholes (see below) (12).

Fretboard or Fingerboard – 4

This is where your fingers press the strings to make different notes and chords. Always finger in the space between the metal frets, not on the metal frets themselves.

Frets – 5

Frets are the actual metal wires that delineate the fret spaces. When we refer to "fret one" we mean the space between the nut and the first fret wire. When we refer to "fret two" we mean the space between the first and second fret wires. Put your fingers in the space, not on the fretwire!

Headstock – 6

Holds the tuning gears (17) which anchor one end of the strings. The other end of the strings, which have a loop, are anchored to the tailpiece (14).

Neck – 7

Connects the headstock with the body of the instrument and holds the fingerboard and strings. "The neck bone's connected to the headstock…"

Nut – 8

The other point, besides the bridge, where the strings rest. The nut sits between the headstock and the end of the fingerboard and is slightly slotted so the strings don't wander. It's usually made of bone or ivory, not macadamia as you might have suspected. Think of the nut as fret zero.

Pick – 9

The pick or plectrum is the little piece of plastic you use to contact the strings when you strum or play single notes to make noise/music. Picks come in a variety of shapes, sizes, and thicknesses. The pick outline shown is actual size and not to scale with the mandolins shown.

Pickguard – 10

A pickguard protects the top of your mandolin from pick scratches and gouging. If you're the energetic emotional type, your mandolin needs a pickguard or it'll dissolve as you play it.

Position Markers – 11

These are the mother-of-pearl or painted dots and decorations on the front and side of the fingerboard which help you tell, at a glance, one fret from another. You'll usually find them on frets five, seven, nine, twelve and fifteen. Fret twelve usually has two. Most mandolins also have markers on the side of the neck so you can tell positions with a side-long glance.

Soundhole – 12

The oval-shaped opening on A-type mandolins. See "F-holes" above.

Strings – 13

If your mandolin is too easy to fret, check to make sure that these have been installed. If they have not, install immediately (loop end to tailpiece, straight end to tuning pegs) before attempting to play! The mandolin has eight strings tuned in pairs to the same pitches as violin strings: E-A-D-G, from highest to lowest pitch, from right to left. Strumming or picking the strings makes them vibrate. These vibrations are in turn amplified by the top of the instrument. (By the way, they're not really strings at all, they're wires.)

Tailpiece and Cover – 14

This is where the loop end of the strings not attached at the head stock are anchored. Strings often rattle and buzz here. To remedy this, weave a thin piece of leather or felt between strings, tailpiece, and tailpiece cover. (Most players I know remove the tailpiece cover and promptly lose it. Somewhere in the universe there's a 6th or 7th dimension chock full of lost tailpiece covers.)

Top or Soundboard – 15

The top is the main vibrating element of the mandolin. It has to be strong enough to survive the tremendous pressure the strings exert on it, while supple enough to easily resonate and amplify the string vibrations. The quality of the top, a trade-off between strength and resonance, most determines the quality of the sound of the instrument.

Truss Rod Cover – 16

Many mandolins have necks reinforced with a metal truss rod. Most of these rods are adjustable (best done by a repair professional) under the truss rod cover, to correct the neck warp that time, weather, and string pressure often cause. The truss rod cover is a plate, usually plastic, which cosmetically covers this adjustment point.

Tuning Gears – 17

Tuning gears tighten or loosen string tension to raise or lower the pitch of the strings to tune the mandolin.

Getting in Tune

Tuning is a skill that you'll perfect over time. It involves matching the sound of the strings to a reference note. This can be any sound source: a tuning fork, a pitch pipe, a piano, the accompanying cassette tape, another mandolin or instrument, an electronic tuner, even a loud electric fan! (Just joking.) Loosening a string lowers its pitch, tightening a string raises its pitch. If you're new to music or the mandolin, you'll probably need the help of an advanced player or teacher to get you started with tuning.

Mandolins have eight strings tuned in pairs to four different pitches. Most people refer to each pair as one string. String 1 (highest pitched and thinnest) is tuned to E, string 2 to A, string 3 to D, and string 4 to G, just like on the violin. If you look a mandolin in the face, as in "The Mandolin and Its Parts" diagram, string 1 (highest pitched and thinnest) is on your right, string 4 (lowest pitched and thickest) is on your left. As you hold the mandolin in playing position, the G string (string four) is closest to your head, the E string (string one) closest to your knee. The diagram below shows where these notes are located on the piano keyboard.

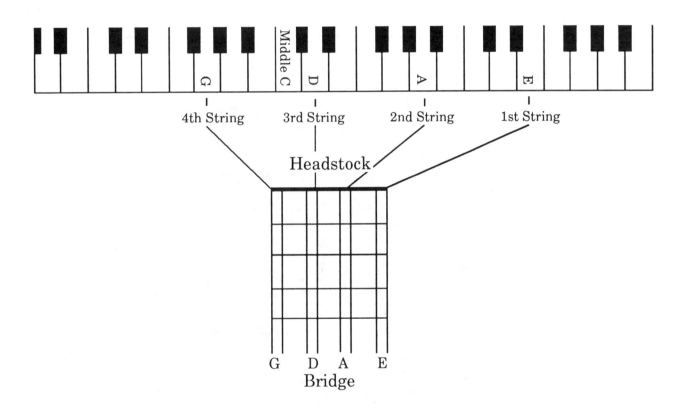

For the purposes of working with this book, I suggest that you tune to the tones at the beginning of the cassette. This will put you in tune with the taped examples and allow you to play along. Some of you lucky souls will have cassette players with speed/pitch controls that allow you to tune the machine to your instrument. Beware though, you'll still have to put your mandolin in tune with itself. Read on.

If you have trouble distinguishing and matching pitches, electronic tuners can help by giving you a visual cue when a string is in tune. This can save you a lot of frustration as you begin developing tuning skills. Just make sure that you don't get addicted to them, or you may never develop the very necessary skill of manual tuning. Also be aware that most electronic tuners are designed to be used with electric instruments. As such, these marvels of computer technology don't usually work well with acoustic mandolins. Try before you buy. If it won't work in the store, it won't work at home or on the gig.

Once you've tuned to the tape or another source, you'll need to fine tune your mandolin to itself. First make sure your fourth string Gs are at the correct source pitch. Fret the fourth string at the seventh fret. Match the sound of the open third string Ds to this pitch by raising or lowering the pitch of the open D strings, not the G. Once that's done you have the G and D strings in tune, fret the third string D at the seventh fret and match the open second string As to it. Finally, fret the second string A at the seventh fret and match the open first string Es to it. Ta-da! All eight strings will be perfectly in tune! Well maybe. Be patient, you'll probably have to practice this a bit.

It's a good idea to check your tuning with this method before each playing session. If your mandolin is impossible to tune, have a repairperson or teacher check to see that your bridge is in the correct spot on the instrument's top. Since it's a floating bridge held in place only by the tension of the strings, it may have moved enough to make tuning difficult.

Illustration copyright 1991, Tom Rozum. Used by permission.

Preparing to Play

First of all, make yourself comfortable in a chair in front of a music stand. Turn the TV off. Use a strap around the neck and shoulder to help support the mandolin. This will help you make your eventual transition to playing while standing easier. (Bluegrassers like to have their straps off one shoulder so they won't have to remove their cowboy hats when they put the mandolin down between sets. While this may be fashion-wise, it often causes tension in the shoulder and picking arm. If you plan to play a lot, use the method that will minimize stress in the long run — over the head with you!) Some teachers, usually classical, suggest using a footstool to raise one knee to support the instrument. Maintaining good posture, both while sitting and standing, is essential to avoid fatigue. See the photos below.

Sitting   *Photo by Al Weiner*

Standing   *Photo by Al Weiner*

What's wrong with this photo?   *Photo by Al Weiner*

You'll need to have a mandolin that plays easily. Romantic legends abound of string greats who started on an instrument made from a cigar box, a Louisville slugger, and barbed wire. They joke about getting slivers from the neck. Forget all that and make sure that the strings are easy to press to the fingerboard. If the *action* (height of the strings above the fingerboard) is high and difficult to finger, it'll just deter your progress.

There are as many different ways to hold the mandolin and pick as there are individual players. The goal is to hold the mandolin and pick in a manner that allows you to reach everything yet won't fatigue your hands. If there is one "correct way," I'm either unaware or suspicious of it. My general suggestion is to hold both the mandolin and pick loosely (they're not very heavy) and do what feels natural. If you have doubts, have a face-to-face consultation with an advanced player or teacher. The photos below show what I do.

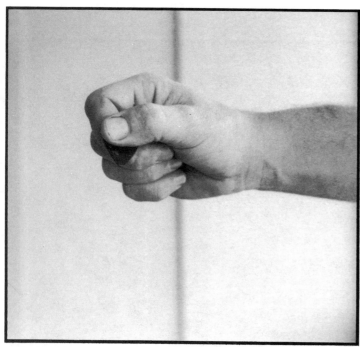

Holding the Pick   *Photo by Al Weiner*   Holding the Mandolin and Pick   *Photo by Al Weiner*

The key to it all — holding, chording, picking, etc. — is to expend only as much energy as is necessary to get the job done. No doubt you'll experience some tenderness on your fingertips as your calluses develop. It's normal, and the more you play, even with the soreness, the quicker calluses will form and soreness will vanish.

Part I — Chords

The first part of this book teaches the fundamental mandolin chords in the context of songs and strums. With just a handful of chords, so to speak, you can play thousands upon thousands of tunes. Of course there are many other chords, variations, and positions that you'll discover as you progress, but right now we want to get you up and playing songs as quickly as possible.

To give you a head start, most of the following are familiar folk songs. Each introduces new chords and strums. You can apply these basics to any style of music. Start shopping now for collections of songs that interest you. The more you like the material, the more you'll play and the faster you'll learn. Choose songbooks that include some type of chord notation, either letters (A, Bm, C7, etc.) or actual diagrams like those shown below. Most pop music songbooks will have guitar chord diagrams, so you'll simply substitute your mandolin A, Bm, C7, etc. chords for the guitar A, Bm, C7, etc. chords. Once you understand how to read chord diagrams (see below), you can look up unknown chords in the back of this book or in a mandolin chord dictionary.

Chord Diagrams

Chord diagrams, like those below, are graphic representations of the mandolin fingerboard. Vertical lines show the strings, 1 to 4, right to left, E to G. (One vertical line represents each string pair.) Horizontal lines represent frets, and the numbers inside the grid show which fingers are used to fret the strings.

We number the fingers of the fretting hand, which for most people will be their left, as follows: 1 – index, 2 – middle, 3 – ring, 4 – pinkie, T – thumb, though you probably won't use the thumb much, if ever, on mandolin. Fret numbers identify both the metal fret wire and the space directly above it on the diagram. Some chord diagrams, like the F below, may have a small letter *x* underneath to denote strings that should not be played. Mute these strings with your fretting hand so they won't sound. (See the photo.) If you can't manage that yet, try to avoid these strings when you strum.

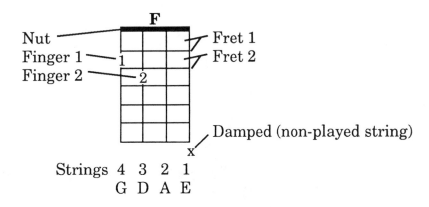

13

Be sure to place your fingers *behind* the metal fret wires as shown, not *on* them. Always use the very *tips* of your fingers straight down on both strings of the pair. This will give you a strong and manageable contact point on the strings. Take care not to bend the first knuckle inward. Let your thumb seek its own natural and comfortable position on the side or back of the neck as you finger different chords.

Fretting with the Fingertips
Photo by Al Weiner

Muting the First String with the Inside of the First Finger
Photo by Al Weiner

Our first two chords, the C and the G (shown below), look quite similar. One could say that they're exactly the same chord played on adjacent strings. This brings up one of the great features of the mandolin. Since its strings are tuned in intervals of perfect fifths, its fingering is symmetrical. Related chords (like the C and the G), melodies, and scales retain their basic positions as you play up and down the neck or across the strings. This makes learning chords and changing keys quite easy. You can usually learn just one hand position and move it to different places on the neck. The guitar, by comparison, is not nearly so regular. Ain't the mandolin wonderful?

C

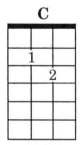

G

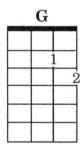

As you first practice these or any new chords, pick each pair of strings individually to isolate any buzzes or dead spots that might arise from improperly placed fingertips. When you hear problems, try adjusting your grip until they are improved. There will be frustrating times when one finger/string combination buzzes. When that's fixed, another string that's supposed to sound is muted. When you correct that, the buzz comes back! Give it some time and effort and eventually you'll discover the right combination of position and pressure to make the chord sound great.

The printed music, detailed in the following example, will show you a song's chords, melody, lyrics, and strum pattern. Below the lyrics you'll find the tablature staff. Later, when we get to note reading, you'll learn how to read both standard notation and tablature. At that point you can come back to any of these tunes and play the melody. If you already know how to read either standard notation or tablature, dive right in and try the melodies in addition to the chords and strums. The boxed section below each song has a short annotated excerpt with tips on melody playing. These will make much more sense after you've worked through Part II. If you're a beginner just learning chords, skip them for now.

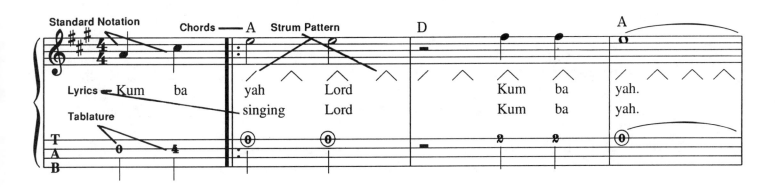

It's important that you work through all the verses to every song as you play along with the tape. Repetition is your best teacher and in no time you'll have the chords memorized. Don't be afraid to sing along, too; it'll make it more fun. No one has to hear but you.

He's Got the Whole World In His Hands

You need to be able to play the C and G chords from memory and switch from one to the other without missing a strum before trying "He's Got the Whole World in His Hands." No doubt you'll have some stray buzzes and mutes, but don't worry too much about that now. The process of playing the chords in a song should help you improve.

"He's Got the Whole World in His Hands" is written in $\frac{4}{4}$ ("four four time"), which means that there are four beats to a measure (top four or numerator of the time signature), and that a quarter note gets one beat (bottom four or denominator of the time signature). To demonstrate this basic rhythm we count or tap our feet to "One, two, three, four" for each measure.

The strum pattern for "He's Got the Whole World in His Hands," as you can hear on the tape, is a basic single downstrum (represented by this symbol: /), one strum per beat, four beats per measure. The entire one-measure strum pattern looks like this: / / / / .

                                                 1 2 3 4

Notice that we don't start our pattern until the first full measure and the lyric "whole world." The lyric "He's got the" falls in an incomplete measure called a *pickup*. More on pickups in Part II.

When chording, the picking hand should pivot slightly at the wrist and move from the elbow. The pick should generally strike the strings at a perpendicular angle. Most players lightly brush the pickguard with the curled fingertips of the picking hand to give them a reference position from which to strum.

Add your own verses to this song. Some of my female mandopals suggest changing the chorus to conform to the gender of the player's deity! Play along with the stereo cassette tape. It can be panned to the right or left to allow you to hear melody or accompaniment separately.

Reminder: The boxed excerpt following the song is for more advanced melody players. If you're a beginner, skip this until you've worked through Part II.

He's Got the Whole World in His Hands

Key of C

whole wide world — in His hands — He's got the whole world
you and me brother — in His hands — He's got — you and me brother
everybody here — in His hands — He's got — everybody here

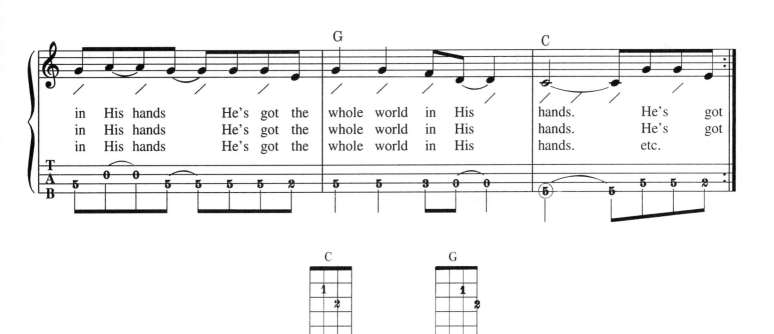

in His hands — He's got the whole world in His — hands. — He's — got
in His hands — He's got the whole world in His — hands. — He's — got
in His hands — He's got the whole world in His — hands. — etc.

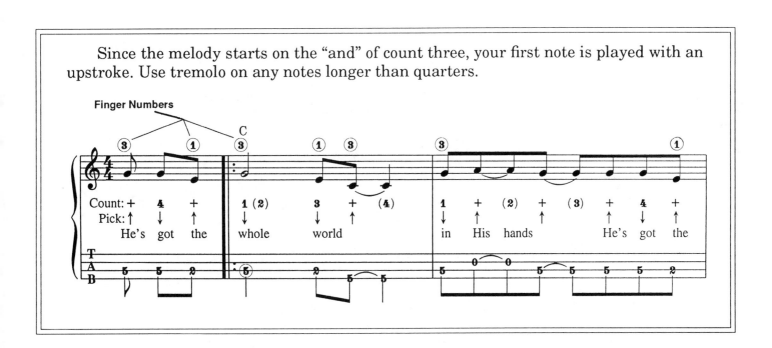

Since the melody starts on the "and" of count three, your first note is played with an upstroke. Use tremolo on any notes longer than quarters.

17

Hush Little Baby

"Hush Little Baby" 's new chords are F and D. The song also has a *modulation* from the key of F to the key of G (after the baby gets the looking glass) to give you practice with more chords and keys.

Different keys give us different pitch ranges in which to perform songs. The melody to "Hush Little Baby" in the key of G is one step higher (equal to an interval of two frets) than it is in the key of F. Once you can perform the tune as written with the modulation, try substituting G chords for Fs and D chords for Cs in the first part to allow you to play the whole tune in the key of G. Write in the substitute chords in pencil. This is called *transposing*. Next try transposing everything back down to the key of F by making the appropriate substitutions; all the G chords become Fs, all the Ds become Cs.

One good use for transposing is to accommodate singers (even yourself!) who need to perform a song in a higher or lower key than written. All you have to do is substitute appropriate chords. See the "Scale, Chord and Transposition Chart" in the back of this book for more information. Use the basic "straight four" all-down strum from "He's Got the Whole World in His Hands." Remember to damp or not strum the first string on the F chord (notice the *x* under the chord diagram).

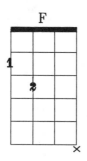
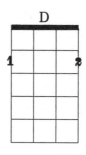

Hush Little Baby

Keys of F and G

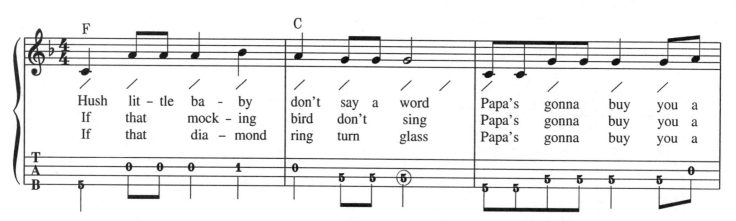

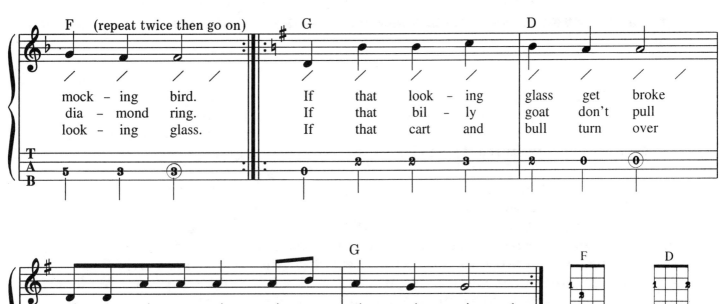

"Hush Little Baby" has lots of eighth notes with down-up (↓ ↑) pick stroke combinations. In the third measure, eighth-note Gs (third string, fifth fret) follow eighth-note Cs (fourth string, fifth fret). Don't lift your third finger to change from the fourth string to the third; rather, use a rolling motion with the finger tip to accomplish the move from string four to string three. It'll save you time and energy.

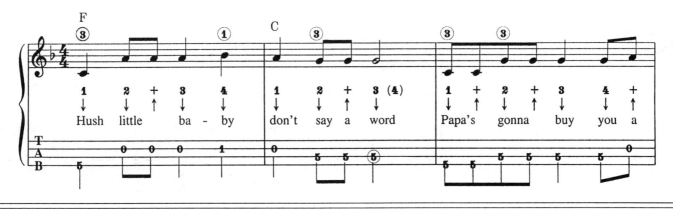

The Streets of Laredo

"The Streets of Laredo" is our first song in waltz or $\frac{3}{4}$ "three-four" time. Instead of counting "One, two, three, four" for each measure as we did in the previous tunes, we count and strum "One-two-three." Waltzes, like "Take Me Out to the Ballgame," "The Tennessee Waltz," or "Brahm's Lullaby" have a definite "three feel" and you almost can't help saying "one-two-three, one-two-three" to yourself as you listen to or play them.

This is also our first song with three chords, including the new A chord below. You'll notice that all four strings are fretted. Since this chord has no open or non-fretted strings, it is in *closed position*. While closed-position chords might be a little more difficult to finger at first, they can be moved up and down the neck to make different chords. ("Up the neck" means moving toward the bridge, raising the pitch; "down the neck" means moving toward the nut, lowering the pitch). For example, if you move the new A chord **down** one fret (one *half step*), toward the nut, it becomes a A♭ (A flat) chord. If you take the same A and move it **up** one fret (one *half step*), toward the bridge, it becomes a B♭ chord. Up two more frets and it becomes a C chord. (All chords using this position are shown in the "Chord Appendix" in the back of the book.) The obvious advantage of this is that it lets you play several different chords with one basic hand position. If you have trouble fingering the chord as shown, try fretting the third string with your second finger.

Measure nine has a dotted quarter note ♩. which gives the melody a bit of a syncopated feel. Listen to the taped example. Keep the strums regular and uniform, though you might be tempted to syncopate along with the melody. We'll discuss dotted notes in more detail in Part II.

The Streets of Laredo

Key of D

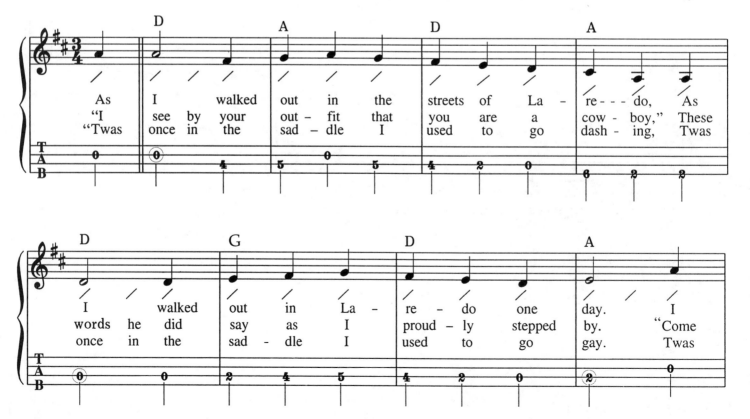

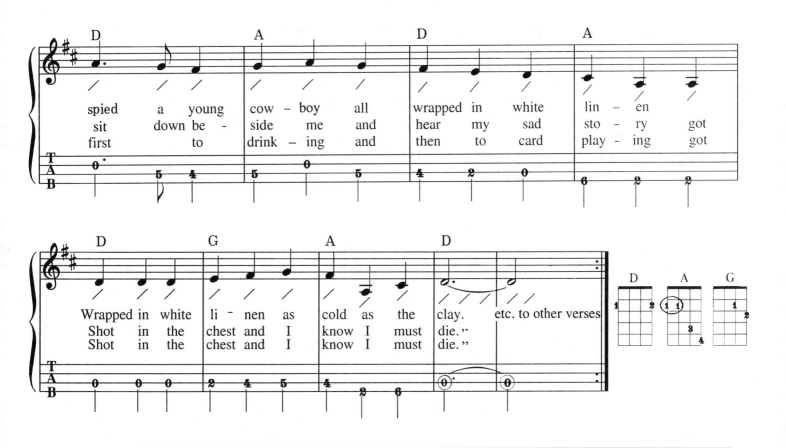

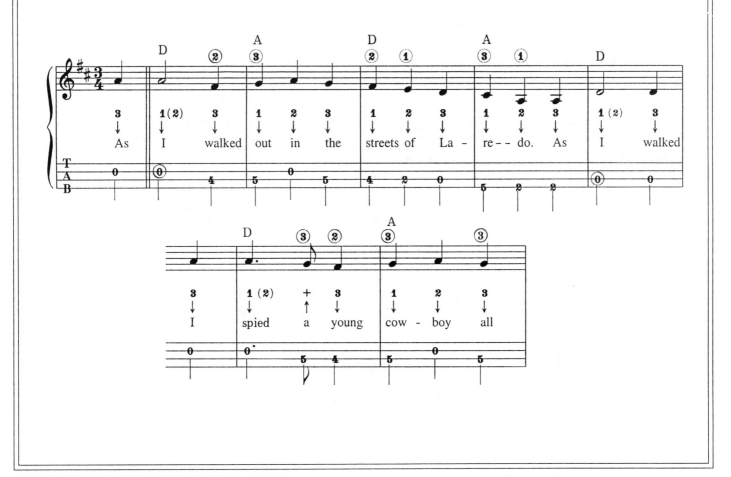

Since almost all of the notes are quarter or half notes, downstrokes prevail. One exception, a dotted quarter followed by an eighth, is in the ninth full measure. Be sure to play the dotted quarter with a downstroke, the eighth with an upstroke.

Kumbaya

On "Kumbaya" we'll learn a new strum pattern, "down, down-up, down-up, down-up," and a new chord, the closed-position E. It's not a particularly easy chord to finger, but give it the old mando-try. Two slightly different fingerings are shown. The first is a bit easier than the second; but, if you have big fat fingers like me, you'll probably have to use the second. If you find both impossible to play, try the third "emergency chord" shown. We'll learn more about these closed-position three-string chords later, but briefly this one is fingered above the fifth fret and the first string is not played.

The "down, down-up, down-up, down-up" strum is counted "One, Two-and, Three-and, Four-and." We still play downstrums on beats one through four but we're adding upstrums in the spaces between two and three, three and four, four and the one of the next measure. We write downstrums as slashes /, upstrums as backslashes \. A down-up strum looks like this: ∧, and the whole pattern looks like this: /   ∧   ∧   ∧.

1 2 and 3 and 4 and

(In Part II we'll discuss up and down picking of single notes represented by arrows ↓ ↑. Slashes refer to strums, arrows to single notes.)

It's important that you practice unfamiliar chords or strums until you have them memorized. If you don't, it'll be nearly impossible to feel the flow of the song as you struggle to remember an A chord or the "down, down-up, down-up, down-up" strum. Of course any of the songs in this book can be played with the single downstrum. If you have trouble integrating the new chords, song, and strum pattern all at once, play the song first with the single downstrum. Eventually though you'll want to learn these different strums to vary your accompaniment and allow you to play a variety of different feels.

In the third measure from the end, you'll have to change chords after only two beats instead of the three or four beats you're used to. Concentrate on even timing. Slow the tempo down until you can change chords easily without slowing down, speeding up, or missing a beat.

Extend "Kumbaya" by adding other verses like "Someone's crying," "Someone's praying," etc., until you give your hands and brain a real workout. Make it a point to play new chords and strums until they become second nature.

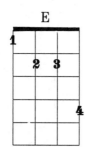
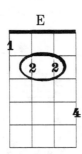
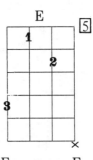

Emergency E Chord

The boxed number to the right of a chord diagram shows where to place the chord on the mandolin fingerboard. In the E above, make the chord *above* the fifth fret wire. Your first finger will be in the sixth fret *space*.

Kumbaya

Like "Streets of Laredo," "Kumbaya" 's melody is made up of mostly quarter or longer notes played with downstrokes. Watch the thirteenth full measure with its eighth and quarter note combination. Notice also the half rest in the second full measure. In the counting line, it's set off with double parentheses (( )). Be sure to keep counting as you rest for two beats.

Measure 13

24

John B. Sails

This old sailing song (a.k.a. "The Sloop John B.") will introduce you to a new chord, the B♭, a new type of chord, the C7 or *dominant seven,* and a new "calypso-style" strum.

Take a look at the B♭ chord. Does it look like one you already know? Right, it's a dead ringer for the closed-position A you used in "Streets of Laredo" and "Kumbaya," except it's one fret higher on the neck. As mentioned before, this is a closed form which can be moved up and down the neck to make different chords. Easy, eh? You'll also notice that the B♭ chord diagram looks slightly different from the others you've seen. Instead of the heavy line signifying the nut at the top of the grid, you find a thinner line and the words "2nd fret." Since we're moving up the neck, we need to shift our perspective on the grid accordingly, and, you guessed it, we fret the chord as shown above the second fret wire. Your first finger will be in the third fret space.

This B♭, like the other chords you've learned so far, is called a *major triad*. Triads contain only three **different** notes (hence the term *tri*-ad). Major triads contain the first, third, and fifth notes of the major scale that names them. For example, the C chord is made up of the notes C, E, and G, from the C major scale:

C	D	E	F	G	A	B	C
1	2	3	4	5	6	7	8

(Notes one and eight are the same note an *octave* apart.) All chords identified by a letter name (C, C♯ or D♭, D, D♯ or E♭, E, F, F♯ or G♭, G, G♯ or A♭, A, A♯ or B♭, B) without other symbols or numbers like m, M7, 13, dim, aug, m6, etc., are major triads. All of the major scales are listed in Part II of this book.

Noting the furrow in your brow, I can see that you are confused. "But," say you, "aren't I playing **four** notes when I strum the C chord? After all, I'm playing all four strings." Right you are. The notes are E (string one open), C (string two fingered at the third fret), E (string three fingered at the second fret), and G (string four open). Four notes, but only three **different** notes since the E note repeats. Mandolin chords often contain repeated notes.

The *dominant seven* chord is closely related to the major triad. You could call them father and son. To make a dominant seven chord we take a basic major triad and add the *flatted* seventh note of the chord's major scale. The C major scale's seventh note is B, which we lower (flat) one half step to become B♭. The C dominant 7 chord (usually called just plain "C seven" and written *C7*) has the notes of the C triad, C, E, and G plus the B♭. The flatted seventh note, the B♭, is played at the third fret of the fourth string.

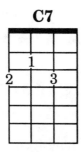

C7

Each type of chord — the triad, dominant seven, minor, diminished, major seven, minor seven, sixth, etc. — has a unique formula which determines which notes from the major scale are played and how the chord is formed on the mandolin.

If you're really on the ball, you're probably saying to yourself, "Hold it right there, bub! You just said that the C7 chord has four notes, C, E, G, and B♭. Where's the G note?" First of all, nobody likes a smart aleck. Second, you're onto something here. Let's look at the C7 chord diagram and figure out which chord notes are where. String one has the E (open), string two has the C (third fret), string three has the E (second fret), and string four has the B♭. No G at all! Many mandolin chords leave out one or more of the chord tones, especially on extended chords with more than four tones. That's OK as long as the "flavor" note that most defines the sound of the chord, in this case the B♭, is still played. It's inevitable with only four strings, something has to give. If you're a purist and insist on having the G note in the chord, try fretting both the first and second strings at the third fret. More on this later.

The strum for "John B. Sails" is "down, down-up, up, down-up,"

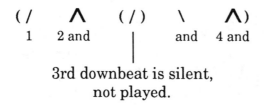

kind of a calypso thing, counted "One, Two-and, -and, Four-and." The absence of the downstroke on the third beat is what gives it that syncopated feel. Here's another way of looking at it:

$$(/ \quad \wedge \quad (/) \quad \backslash \quad \wedge)$$
$$1 \quad 2 \text{ and} \quad \quad \text{and} \quad 4 \text{ and}$$

3rd downbeat is silent,
not played.

John B. Sails

Key of F

Remember the calypso strum you learned for "John B. Sails" with its emphasis on upstrokes? The melody is structured the same way and should have the same feel. Pay close attention to pick direction.

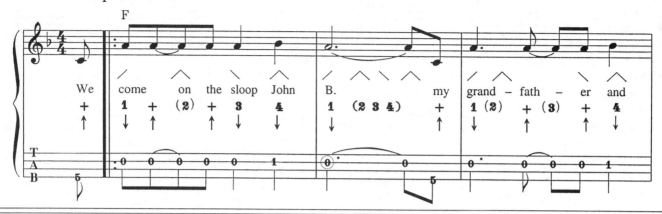

Gibson "A"

Photo by Dix Bruce, © Copyright 1982

I Ride An Old Paint

"I Ride an Old Paint," like "The Streets of Laredo," is a cowboy waltz, counted "One, Two, Three; One, Two, Three" (two measures).

If you've been paying attention, you're probably about to complain that you've "already learned *one* B♭ chord in 'John B. Sails.' How come I gotta learn another one?" When you're older you'll understand.

Didn't buy that, eh? As I mentioned earlier, there are several ways to finger any given chord on the mandolin. Take a quick peek at the "Chord Appendix" at the back of the book to see what I mean. Each sounds unique and occurs at a different position on the mandolin neck. Knowing more than one offers you a choice of musical colors and the ability to play a chord at several locations on the fingerboard. This latter advantage saves unnecessary hand movement.

OK, I admit it, the new B♭ is one tough cookie for you people with normal, human-sized fingers. Down by the bunk house we call it "The Fingerbuster." But, trust me on this, it's one of the most useful forms you'll ever learn. It's commonly called "the bluegrass chop" or long form and, you guessed it, it's very popular with bluegrassers. Like the new F7, this new B♭ is a closed-position, moveable chord. If your fingers just flat-out refuse to contort to this degree, you have my permission to use the B♭ chord from "John B. Sails," but only temporarily! In the meantime work on getting your fingers used to the stretch by holding and releasing the chord about fifty times each day. Someday you'll thank me. Try to find a comfortable position for your wrist and relax it between strums if you can.

The new F7 form is fingered just like the C7 you learned in "John B. Sails" but moved five frets up the neck. Like the F chord you already know, the new F7 has a little *x* under the first string. Unlike the C7 or the other four-string chords you've learned, this F7 is a *three-string chord* since the first string is not played.

We know from the dominant seven formula that the F7 chord has the notes F, A, C, and E♭ (one, three, five, and flat seven of the F major scale), but this F7 leaves out the C note (the five of the chord)! We could add a C (on the first string, fifth fret) as we discussed with the C7 in "John B. Sails," but we can get away without it since the chord's main flavor note, the E♭ or flatted seven, is present on the fourth string, eighth fret. Why leave the C (or the 5 of the chord) out? It gives us a distinctive sound, one that really emphasizes the flatted seven.

The easiest way *not* to play the first string on this chord is to damp it slightly with the inside of your fretting hand. (I use that extra blob of skin that bunches up near the first knuckle when I finger the chord. Review the photo on page 14.) Experiment to discover the correct amount of pressure to mute just the first strings without buzzes or damping of the other strings.

The strum for "I Ride an Old Paint" is quite easy; it uses the basic downstroke pattern and adds an upstroke to the "and" of beat number two; "down, down-up, down" (/ ⋀ /) counted "One, Two-and, Three."

1 2 and 3

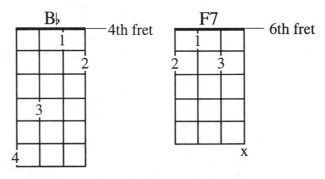

I Ride an Old Paint

Key of B♭

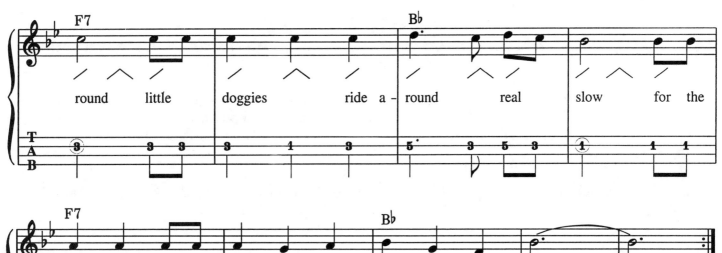

round little doggies ride a - round real slow for the

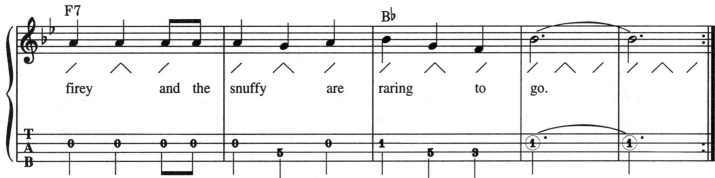

firey and the snuffy are raring to go.

The tricky part to "Old Paint" is the dotted quarter/eighth combination. It's easy if you pay attention the counting and pick direction.

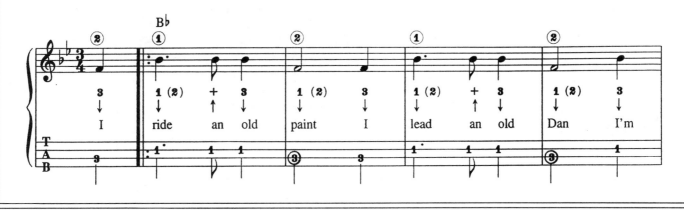

I ride an old paint I lead an old Dan I'm

Careless Love

"Careless Love," an old folk blues, has a new G7 and a new closed-position G chord, the same form as the B♭ from "Old Paint" played three frets (1½ steps) lower on the neck. The strum is "down, down-up, down-up, down" (/ ∧ ∧ /) and counted "One, Two-and, Three-and, Four."
                                1 2 and 3 and 4

The new G7 form below is another three-string chord with a damped first string (check the x under the grid). Since it's a dominant seven chord, it should have the notes

$$\begin{array}{cccc} G & B & D & F \\ 1 & 3 & 5 & \flat 7 \end{array}$$

but this G7 chord has no G at all! Once again we're leaving out a chord note, this time the root or "one" of the chord. Again, we could add a G note (on the first string, third fret) but we can get away without it since the chord's main flavor note, the F or flatted seven, is present on the third string, third fret. Why leave the G (or the one of the chord) out? Just like the three-string F7 in "I Ride An Old Paint," this chord gives us a different sound, one that really emphasizes the flatted seven. Three- and four-string versions of the same chord, like different positions, have slightly different sounds and uses. Of course, it's up to you to decide where to use them. While we're on the subject, try the slightly different closed-position C chord shown below.

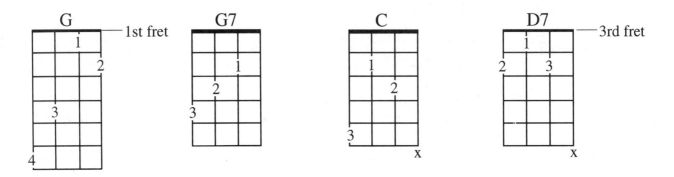

The strum is "down, down-up, down-up, down," (/ ∧ ∧ /),
                                        1 2 and 3 and 4

which is counted "One, Two-and, Three-and, Four." By now you've mastered quite a few different strums. As you've probably already realized, you can substitute one for another. Of course, you have to be careful when you use a waltz strum ("One, Two, Three") on a four-beat tune or vice versa. Most of the time it just won't fit. There are exceptions (see "Sportin' Life.") As you learn new strums, go back and try them on the songs and chords you already know.

Try the strums you already know on "Careless Love." Don't be afraid to mix different strums together in one song as we'll do later on "Fair and Tender Ladies." Try looking ahead in the book and playing chords along with the tape on songs you'll learn in Part II.

Careless Love

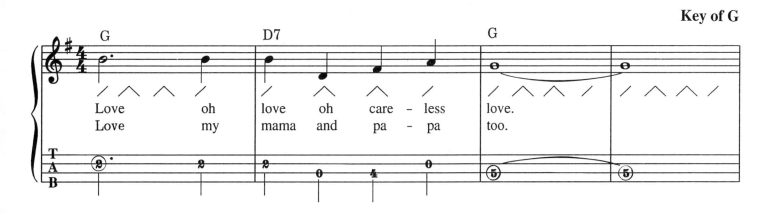

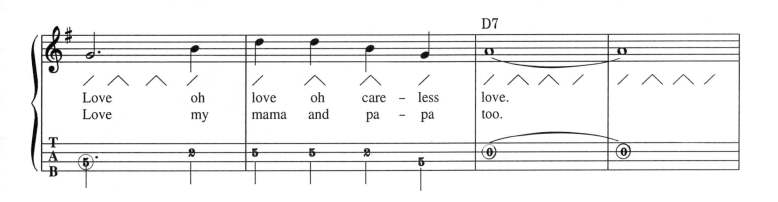

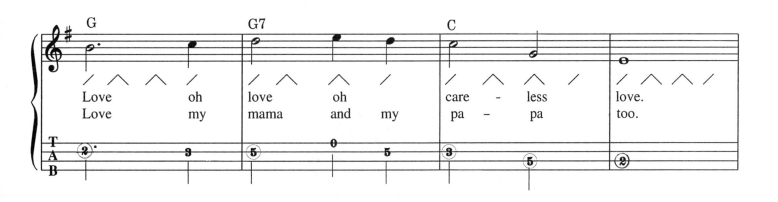

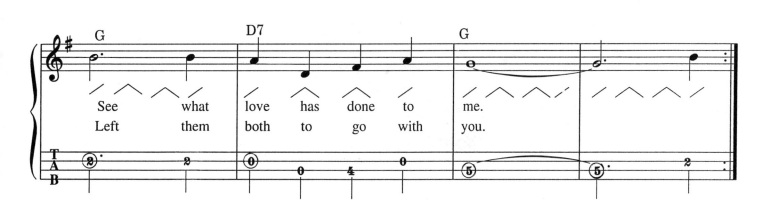

"Careless Love" is quite straightforward with lots of opportunities to practice your tremolo.

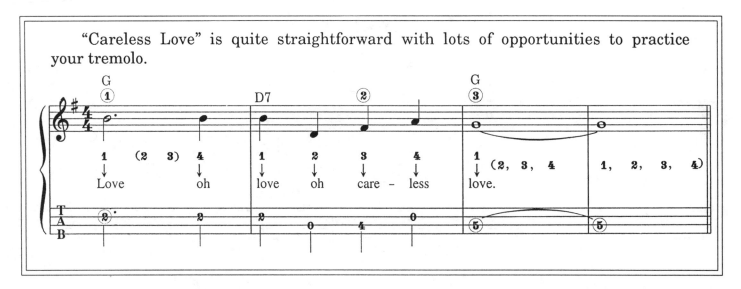

The Stelling

Sportin' Life

So far you've learned two types of chords — triads and dominant sevens — and the formulas that determine how they are fingered on the mandolin. As you know, there are many other types (minor, ninth, major seven, diminished, augmented, etc.) and each chord has its own sound and function, like words in your musical vocabulary.

To a beginner it can seem like a staggering amount of material to memorize. My advice is to learn chords a few at a time in the context of songs. That allows you to build a repertoire of chords (which you can apply to other new songs) as you learn songs. If you come across a chord that you don't know, look it up in the back of this book or in a chord dictionary. Don't bother memorizing chords abstractly; it's not much fun and thus not a particularly good way to learn.

"Sportin' Life" is something of a quantum leap into intermediate beginnerhood and explores challenging new material on several fronts. (However, if you're like me, half Norwegian and pulsing with that hot Nordic blood, you have a special feeling for the blues and will want to leap right in on whatever level your abilities allow.) It includes two new types of chords, *minor* and *diminished*, some new positions for chords you already know, and uses a triplet strum. Any of these could cause you serious grief if you expect to master them immediately. My advice is to learn the chords first and get comfortable playing along with the tape before you tackle the new chord positions and strum. Of course, you'll have to learn a few brand-new chords to get through it. Take it at your own speed and try to understand the theory behind the finger moves.

Minor and diminished chords are closely related to each other and to major triads. As you know, a major triad, like the C, G, F, and D chords you've learned, is made up of the one, three, and five of the chord's major scale. The A major scale is:

A	B	C♯	D	E	F♯	G♯	A
1	2	3	4	5	6	7	8

So the A chord is made up of the notes A, C♯, and E.

A *minor* triad is made up of the one, *flat-three,* and five of the chord's major scale, only one note different (*flat-three* instead of *natural three*) from the major triad. To flat the three, we lower it one half step (one fret), just like we did with the flat seven in the dominant seven chord. If we flat the C♯ note of the A chord, it becomes a C *natural*, and the chord changes from A to A minor (Am) with the notes A, C natural, and E. You could say that the minor and major triads are first cousins.

The Am chord in "Sportin' Life" is quite a stretch, another "Fingerbuster," but you'll find that it's very convenient after the closed-position A that precedes it. To get from A to Am, all you have to do is move your index finger down one fret! (You're probably cursing me under your breath and repeating the old saw "easier said than done.") Of course, you could use the alternate A and Am chords shown. While these offer the same advantage of moving only one finger to get from the A to the Am and back, you've got quite a jump to the chords that come before and after. The big jumps are what we want to avoid wherever possible. I had that in mind when I arranged "Sportin' Life." As you play through it, you'll see that all the chords fall into one general region of the fingerboard.

The *diminished seven* is derived directly from the other chords you've already studied, cousins once again. Before we get to it, though, let's look at the *diminished triad*, which is slightly different from the diminished seven. Diminished chords, whether diminished triads or diminished sevens, are noted with a small circle following the letter name of the chord, e.g., C°, F°7, A♭°, etc.

The diminished triad is made up of the one, flat-three, and *flat-five* of its major scale. If you take a minor triad (one, flat-three, five of the corresponding major scale) and flat the five, *presto!* You've got a diminished triad. For example, the C major scale is:

C	D	E	F	G	A	B	C
1	2	3	4	5	6	7	8

The C diminished triad has the notes are C, E♭, and G♭.

The diminished seven chord, sometimes called the *fully diminished*, uses the one, flat-three, flat-five, and *flatted* flat-seven of its major scale. For C°7 the notes are C, E♭, G♭, and B♭♭ or A. You can think of the diminished seven as a third cousin of the dominant seven with three different (flatted) notes. Take any dominant seven and flat its three, five, and flat-seven, and you'll end up with a diminished seven chord. In "Sportin' Life" we have the A♯°7 (a.k.a. B♭°7) with the notes A♯, C♯, E, and G (or B♭, D♭, F♭, and A♭♭).

"A♯°7" and "B♭°7" are *enharmonic spellings* or names for the same chord. That's because A♯ and B♭ are *enharmonic spellings* for the same note. Look at the piano keyboard below.

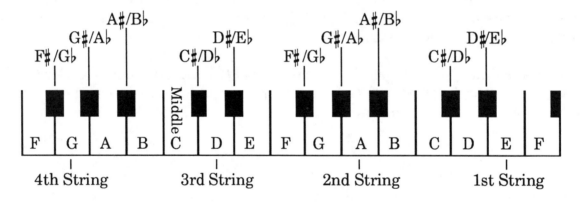

Each note, white and black, is one half step from its neighbor. The next note up from a G can either be called a G♯ or an A♭. The appropriateness of one name or the other depends on the context in which you are referring to the note or chord. For example, when we *flat* a note, like the third of a C triad to make it a C minor triad, we go from E to E♭. It makes more sense to call the flatted note "E flat" than "D sharp" because we've "flatted" the E, not "sharped" the D. By the same token if we *sharp* the five of a G triad (G, B and D) it makes more sense to call the new note "D sharp" rather than "E flat."

In the B♭°7 chord listed above you'll notice two weird notes, F♭ ("F flat") and A♭♭ ("A double flat"). While these are technically correct, they're somewhat cumbersome and confusing. Most people call F♭ an E and C♭ a B. If we flat an already flatted note, as with A♭♭, we usually refer to it as the next logical note, in this case G natural. It takes some time to get the hang of the nomenclature and there are other rules/opinions that I won't tax you with here. No doubt you'll run up against a snooty know-it-all who'll share the rules with you soon enough.

One great thing about diminished seven chords is that they can be named by any note in the chord. Thus a C°7, which has the notes C, E♭, G♭, and A, is also an E♭°7, G♭°7, or A°7. Anytime you're asked for one, you can play any of the four, since they're the same chord. Same with the C♯°7 (with the notes C♯, E, G, and B♭) and the D°7 (with the notes D, F, G♯, and B). Since those three chords contain all the notes (C, C♯/D♭, D, D♯/E♭, E, F, F♯/G♭, G, G♯/A♭, A, A♯/B♭, B), you really have to learn only three different diminished seven chords! That gives you a one-in-three chance of getting any diminished seven chord correct.

The strum for "Sportin' Life" superimposes a waltz on a straight four framework. Instead of counting "One, two, three, four" for each measure, we count "One, two, three; Two, two, three; Three, two, three; Four, two, three" and play three downstrokes on each of the four beats in the measure. This strum will be noted in the tablature line with the numeral "3." The whole pattern looks like this:

$$
\begin{array}{cccc}
3 & 3 & 3 & 3 \\
123 & 223 & 323 & 423
\end{array}
$$

It's a lot of downstrokes, so keep the tempo slow enough to comfortably fit them all in.

Practice the several new three-string chords before you try to play the song. The next-to-the-last measure has an embarrassment of chord changes, one per beat. Don't panic; remember that the strum is in triplets, so you'll still get to strum three times on each chord.

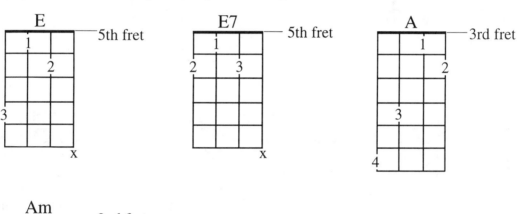

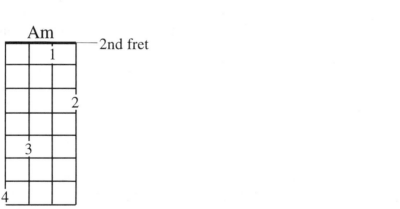

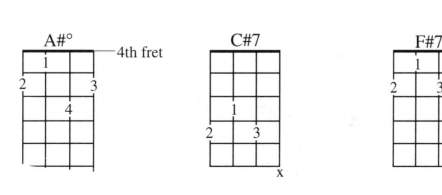

37

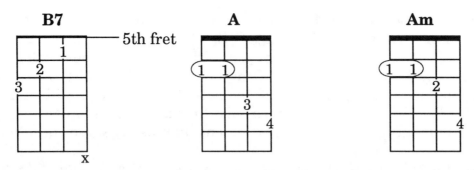

Alternate A & Am
(First finger has to negotiate two strings!)

Sportin' Life

I'm get – ting tired of runnin' 'round, think I'll get
letter from home, most of my
gambler a cheater too, but now it's

married and I'll settle down, You know that old nightlife that old
friends are dead and gone, You know that old nightlife that old
come my turn to lose, You know that sportin' life is holding the

sportin' life is killin' me. I got a
sportin' life is killin' me. I been a
best hand, what can I do?

38

One final note on "Sportin' Life." The chord progression in the fifth and sixth measures (E, C♯7, F♯7, B7) is often referred to as a *"one-six-two-five progression"* since the chords are based on the one, six, two and five of the E major scale. The E major scale is

E	F♯	G♯	A	B	C♯	D♯	E
1	2	3	4	5	6	7	8

In this case all are major or dominant seven chords, though you'll often see minors, especially on the two and six chords. One-six-two-five progressions form the backbone of most of the pop and jazz repertoire. Learn 'em! We'll get into more detail on one-six-two-fives with "The Cruel War."

People often refer to this type of blues as having a "6/8" or "triplet" feel. The traditional way to play this feel is with all downstrokes. In the first full measure, you can roll your first finger from the second to the third strings, just like in "Hush Little Baby."

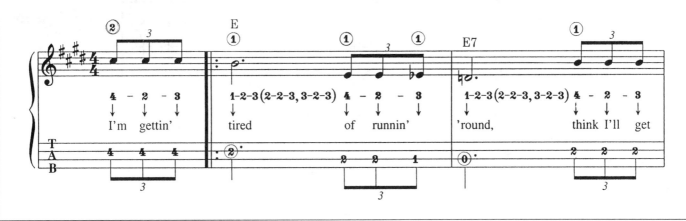

Fair and Tender Ladies

"Fair and Tender Ladies" is such a pretty song I just had to include it! This version gives you practice on a strum pattern which combines two others, "down, down-up, down-up, down-up," and "down, down, down, down,"

$$(/\ \wedge\ \wedge\ \wedge,\ /\ /\ /\ /)$$
1 2 and 3 and 4 and, 1 2 3 4

to make a two-measure pattern. You'll also work with different positions for the D chord and learn a closed-position Em chord.

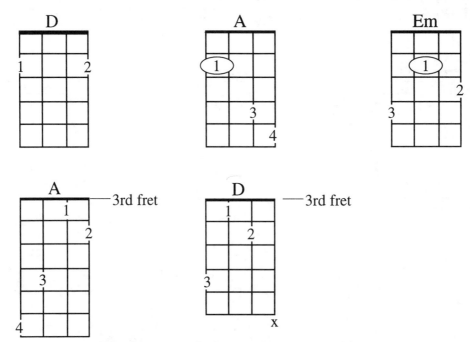

Fair and Tender Ladies

Key of D

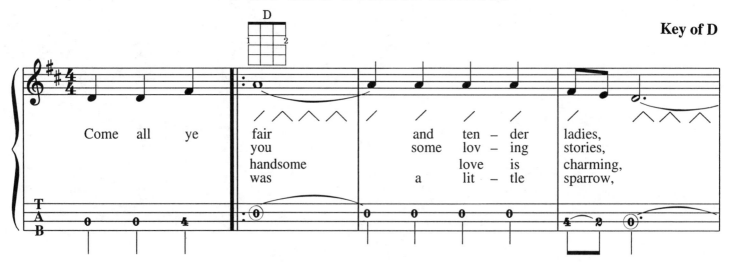

Come all ye | fair | and ten – der | ladies,
 | you | some lov – ing | stories,
 | handsome | love is | charming,
 | was | a lit – tle | sparrow,

41

"Fair and Tender Ladies" is loaded with long tied notes. As such, it's great for practicing your tremolo. Don't miss the pull-offs in the third and fifteenth full measures.

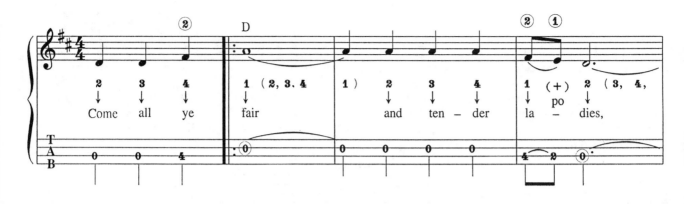

Gibson A, ca. 1924   *Photo by Dix Bruce © Copyright 1982*

The Cuckoo

Up to this point all the songs have been in major keys, beginning and ending on major chords. Right away you'll notice that "The Cuckoo" is different and has a slightly melancholy sound because of the G minor chords. This tonality is often referred to as *G-modal* or *G-dorian*. (For more information on keys and modes, consult a music theory text. I've listed two in the "Sources" section in the back of this book.)

All the chords in "The Cuckoo" have open strings and are not moveable. Now that you're an experienced and sophisticated mandolinist, you probably think open-string chords are low tech, even passe. Not so! The bottom line here is sound, right? Strum the Gm chord. Doesn't it have a beautiful ringing tone? You can't get that exact sound with a closed-string chord. Don't rule a chord out because it's "simple." Sounds paint pictures, and chords are your colors. Learn how each chord sounds, and use it artistically.

OK, that was my artistic muse speaking. Here comes my practical, educational muse, if there is such a thing. Once you can play "The Cuckoo" with the open chords shown, try it with closed positions. It's up to you to figure them out. Here are some big hints: Try sliding the Am from "Sportin" Life" down two frets to Gm (be forewarned, it's really tough!), try sliding the closed-position E from "Sportin' Life" up one fret to F, slide the F7 from "I Ride An Old Paint" down three frets for the D7. Make chord diagrams of these new chords. Use a "down, down, down-up, down" (**/ / ∧ /**) strum pattern. How would you count this pattern?

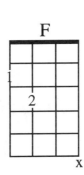

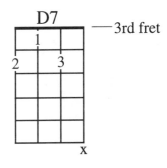

43

The Cuckoo

Oh the cuckoo she's a pretty bird, And she
Diamonds Jack of Dia – monds I
build me log ca – bin On the

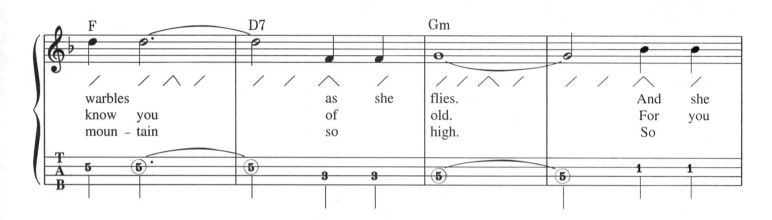

warbles as she flies. And she
know you of old. For you
moun – tain so high. So

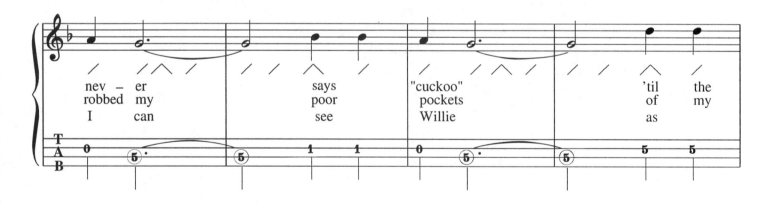

nev – er says "cuckoo" 'til the
robbed my poor pockets of my
I can see Willie as

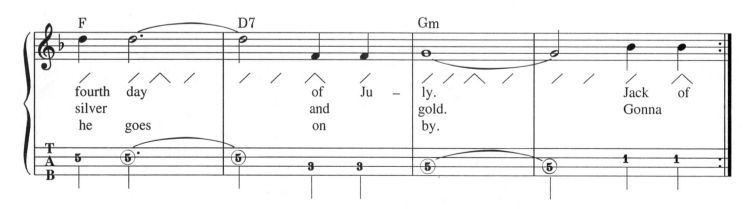

fourth day of Ju – ly. Jack of
silver and on gold. Gonna
he goes on by.

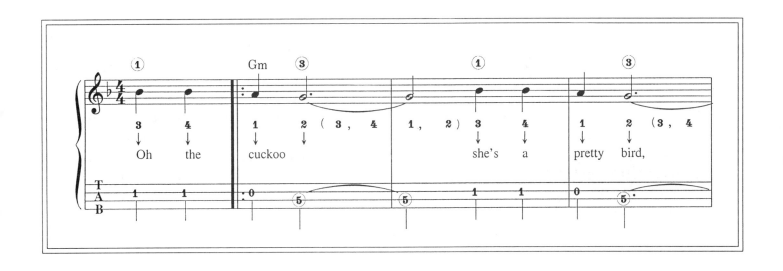

The Flintstone by John Gonder   *Photo by Dix Bruce © Copyright 1982*

The Cruel War

The first four measures of "The Cruel War" use a minor version of the one, six ,two five progression (often noted with the Roman numerals I vi ii V). You saw a major version in "Sportin' Life." Roman numerals usually refer to chords in the context of a key. These chords are based on the notes of the major scale which are usually denoted with Arabic numerals. Here's the C major scale:

C	D	E	F	G	A	B	C
1	2	3	4	5	6	7	8

The C note is the "one" of the C scale, the F is the "four," etc. It gets confusing when we switch to a chordal context. Here are the chords of the C major scale with their corresponding Roman numerals below:

C	Dm	Em	F	Gm	Am	B°	C
I	ii	iii	IV	V	vi	vii	VIII

Uppercase Roman numerals refer to major chords, lowercase to minor chords, except the vii, which is diminished. All are triads. Each major key has a different set of chords determined by its major scale, though each preserves the pattern of I ii iii IV V vi vii VIII. The IV chord of the key of G major is C, in the key of D the IV is G, in F it's B♭, etc. All this information is detailed in the "Scale, Chord, and Transposition Chart" at the back of this book. For more info on this part of music theory, consult any standard music theory text.

You're probably wondering why you even need to worry about all these confusing numbers. First of all, most pop, folk, country, rock, and bluegrass songs tend to follow one of a handful of standard chord progressions. Musicians can communicate these quickly, clearly, and easily in one phrase like "one, five" ("Old Paint"), "one, five, one, four, one, five, one" ("John B. Sails"), or "one, six, two, five" ("The Cruel War"). Secondly, if you learn this numerical approach and understand where chords occur in keys, you can identify these types of progressions and easily transpose any song to any key to accommodate different voices or playing partners. You'll also find that numbers like "one, six, two, five" shouted across a stage in a noisy bar will be much more easily understood than the sound alikes "Geeeee! Eeeeee! Aaaaay! Deeeee!," especially if you have some bizarre regional accent.

The strum you'll use, "down, down-up, up, down" (/ ∧ \ /), is a variation on the calypso strum from "John B. Sails." On the second beat, a downstroke, emphasize the separate notes of the chord and let them sound individually. This is called *arpeggiating* the chord. Strums sound all the notes of the chord at the same time.

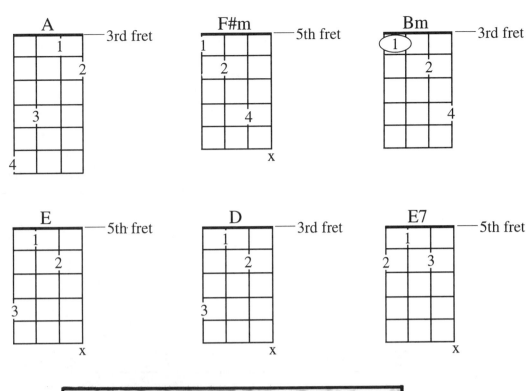

A — 3rd fret

F#m — 5th fret

Bm — 3rd fret

E — 5th fret

D — 3rd fret

E7 — 5th fret

Frank Wakefield's Lloyd Loar Gibson F-5   *Photo by Dix Bruce © 1982*

The Cruel War

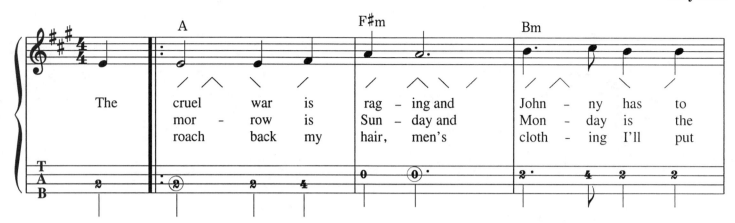

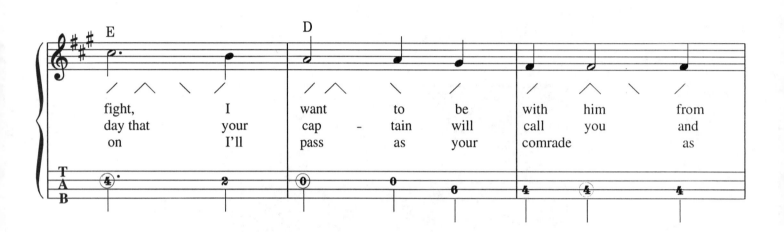

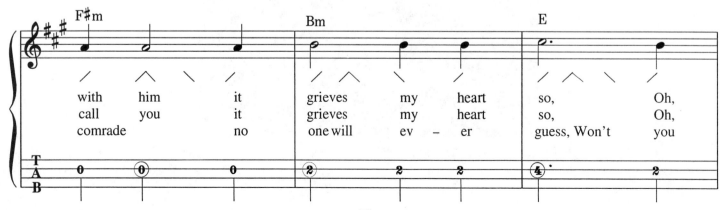

48

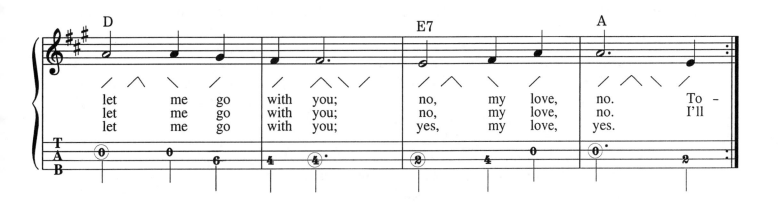

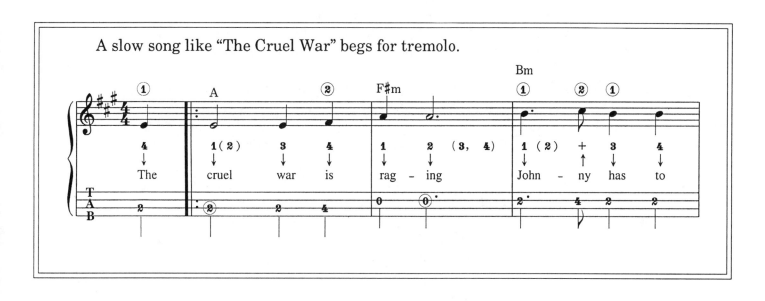

A slow song like "The Cruel War" begs for tremolo.

Nine Pound Hammer

With "Nine Pound Hammer" we step into the bluegrass. Bluegrass music was pioneered by mandolinist Bill Monroe in the late 1930s and early 1940s. Today bluegrass is a separate branch of country music enjoyed by millions around the world. Bluegrass showcases lead and rhythm mandolin playing more than any other music.

In "Nine Pound Hammer" we'll look at the bluegrass mandolin *chop* chord. If you listen to Bill Monroe you'll hear his rhythm playing take a very prominent role, quite a bit like a drummer. His *backbeats* (on beats two and four in $\frac{4}{4}$, beats two and three in $\frac{3}{4}$) infuse the music with an intense energy that propels the whole band. The chords used to create this effect are the closed-position, moveable chords with which you've been working. Bluegrass mandolinists strum these chords and then loosen their fretting-hand grip to damp the sound. The result is a non-ringing, percussive *chopped* sound, hence the name.

The strum you'll use on this and most bluegrass tunes requires that you play only on the backbeats, beats two and four. In the strum line you'll see rests on beats one and three. In a bluegrass band, the bass and guitar would play the downbeats on one and three while you rest. If you're practicing the bluegrass chop by yourself, be sure to add slight downbeats by lightly strumming the fourth string. Otherwise it won't make sense and you won't get the feel of the push and pull, the "boom and chick" of bluegrass rhythm. Listen to the demonstration on the tape and be sure to listen to bluegrass live and on record.

This version of "Nine Pound Hammer" is written in the key of A♭, which is somewhat unusual among bluegrass players who favor sharp keys like G, D, A, etc. You'll be way ahead of them with your facility in A♭. Notice how all the chords fall into one small region of the mandolin neck. Your fretting hand hardly has to move at all. Once you can play "Nine Pound Hammer" as written, try sliding the whole thing up one fret (one half step) to the key of A. The A♭s will become As, the D♭s become Ds, the E♭s become Es. Write these new chords in pencil above the given chords. Don't think about keys, chords, or melody now; concentrate on maintaining that basic hand position. Once you can play the chords in A, slide the whole thing down two frets (one whole step) to the key of G. Neat trick, huh? As you already know, closed-position chords can be moved anywhere up and down the neck. Use the "Scale, Chord, and Transposition Chart" in the back of the book for reference.

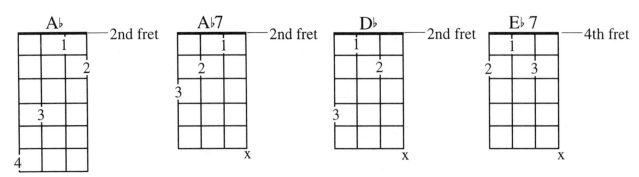

Nine Pound Hammer

Key of A♭

Probably the most challenging part of "Nine Pound Hammer" will be playing in the key of A♭, where you'll have very few open (not fretted) notes. Your fourth finger will get a workout and wish that it had never been born! In the eighth full measure, you'll roll your fourth finger over from the third string to the second string. You'll also have to pay attention to the different eighth and quarter combinations and ties, pick direction, and tremolo on the longer notes. Since the song is usually performed at a fast tempo, increase the speed of your tremolo accordingly.

Photo by Dix Bruce © Copyright 1990

Take a Drink on Me

"Take a Drink on Me" is an old folk blues song. This version is modernized with a bluegrass rhythm part and a *one, six, two, five* (I, VI, II, V) chord progression.

Use bluegrass chop chords on two and four all the way through. Try transposing this to as many other keys as you can think of. Use the transposition chart at the back of the book. Try substituting regular major chords for the dominant sevens written. Listen to the different sounds between major and dominant seven chords.

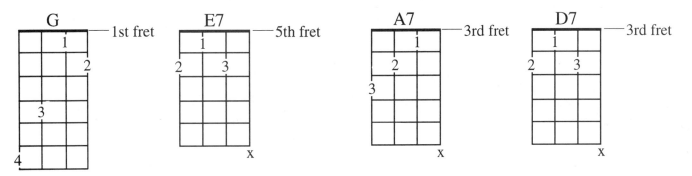

Gibson Style A (top) and F-4 (bottom)

Photo by Dix Bruce © Copyright 1983

53

Take a Drink on Me

Key of G

Swing the rhythm of this one.

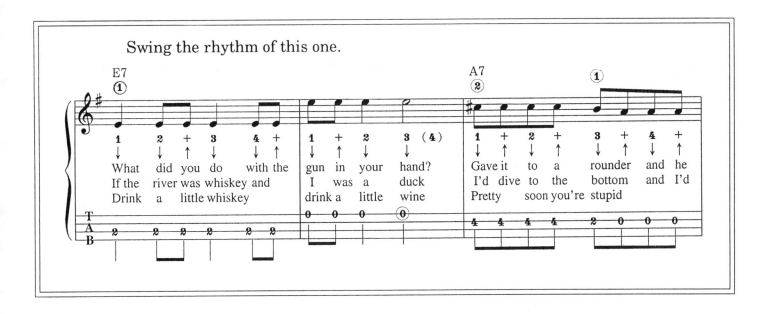

What did you do with the gun in your hand? Gave it to a rounder and he
If the river was whiskey and I was a duck I'd dive to the bottom and I'd
Drink a little whiskey drink a little wine Pretty soon you're stupid

This concludes the chord section of the book. On to note reading!

Mandolin Duets

Copyright 1991, Tom Rozum. Used by permission.

Notes on the Mandolin

Now that you know quite a few chords, strums, and songs, it's time for a brief introduction to notes and note reading. As mentioned before, this book is meant to be an overview rather than a complete text, and as such we'll only outline the subject. For graded lessons on music reading and playing, choose one of the methods listed in the "Sources" section at the end of the book.

Written music communicates two things to the reader/player: *pitch* and *rhythm*. Pitch tells us which sound or note to play, high or low. Rhythm tells us how long to hold that pitch. The result, hopefully, is beautiful music.

Notes for the mandolin are written on a *staff* called the *treble clef,* which is identified by the *treble clef sign.*

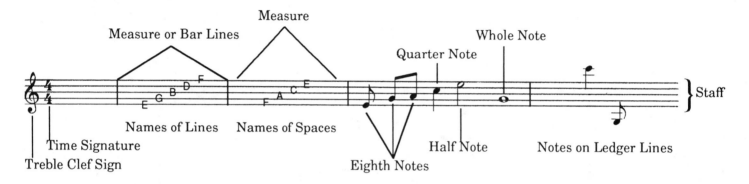

The staff has five lines and four spaces and each represents a different note. The notes on the lines, bottom to top, are E, G, B, D, and F and can be remembered with the phrase "<u>E</u>very <u>G</u>ood <u>B</u>oy <u>D</u>oes <u>F</u>ine." The notes on the spaces, bottom to top, are F, A, C, and E and spell out the word "<u>FACE</u>." (You could, of course, make up your own words or phrases to remember the names of the lines and spaces, even in reverse order. For some reason my "<u>F</u>inley <u>D</u>oesn't <u>B</u>ake <u>G</u>ood <u>E</u>els" and "<u>ECAF</u>" never caught on. Go figure.)

Notes on the staff (line, space, line, space, etc.) ascend alphabetically A to G. They descend in reverse alphabetical order. If you know any note on a line or space, you can name any other by simply following up or down in alphabetical order.

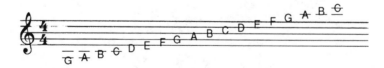

Notes higher or lower than those on the staff are placed on extensions called *ledger lines.* Notes on ledger lines continue the alphabetical pattern above and below the staff.

As you remember from the tuning section at the beginning of this book, open or unfretted strings on the mandolin are tuned to the notes E (string 1 – highest pitched), A (string 2), D (string 3) and G (string 4 – lowest pitched). The diagram below shows where these notes are placed on the staff.

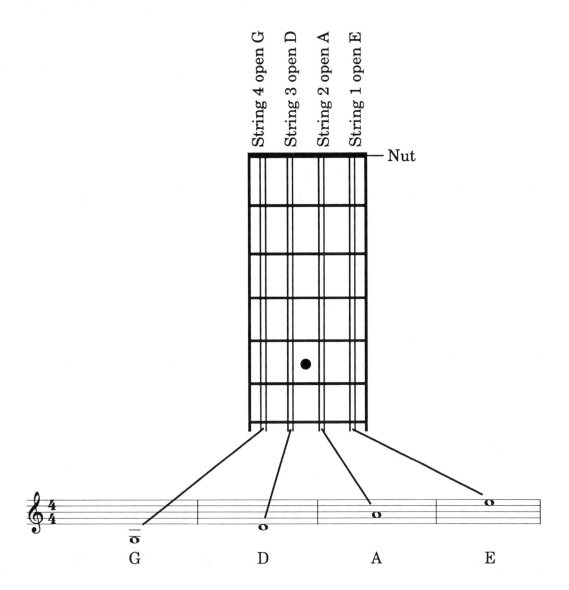

Other notes are made by fingering the strings at the different frets. The range of the mandolin is about three and one half octaves from the open fourth-string G to the twentieth-fret, first-string C. An octave is the interval from one note to the next occurrence of the same note above or below; for example, from the mandolin's open fourth-string G to the next G at the third string, fifth fret. In a major scale it's the distance from note 1 to note 8, or twelve half steps. Your mandolin may have a few notes more or less depending upon the length of your fingerboard and the number of reachable frets.

The following staff and fret chart show where every note on the four strings is located. Study a section of four or five frets at a time and familiarize yourself with the notes on every string. Try to relate each fret/string combination both with a line or space and a letter name. Play the note, repeat its position (e.g., "first string, second fret"), then name it ("F sharp"). By the way, a sharp sign (♯) before a note raises the pitch of that note one half step or one fret. A flat sign (♭) before a note lowers it one half step or one fret. A sharp or flat sign on a line or space applies to every note on that line or space after the sign and before the next bar line. Notes in following measures are unaffected. Sharps and flats, called accidentals, are also used in key signatures. More on that coming up.

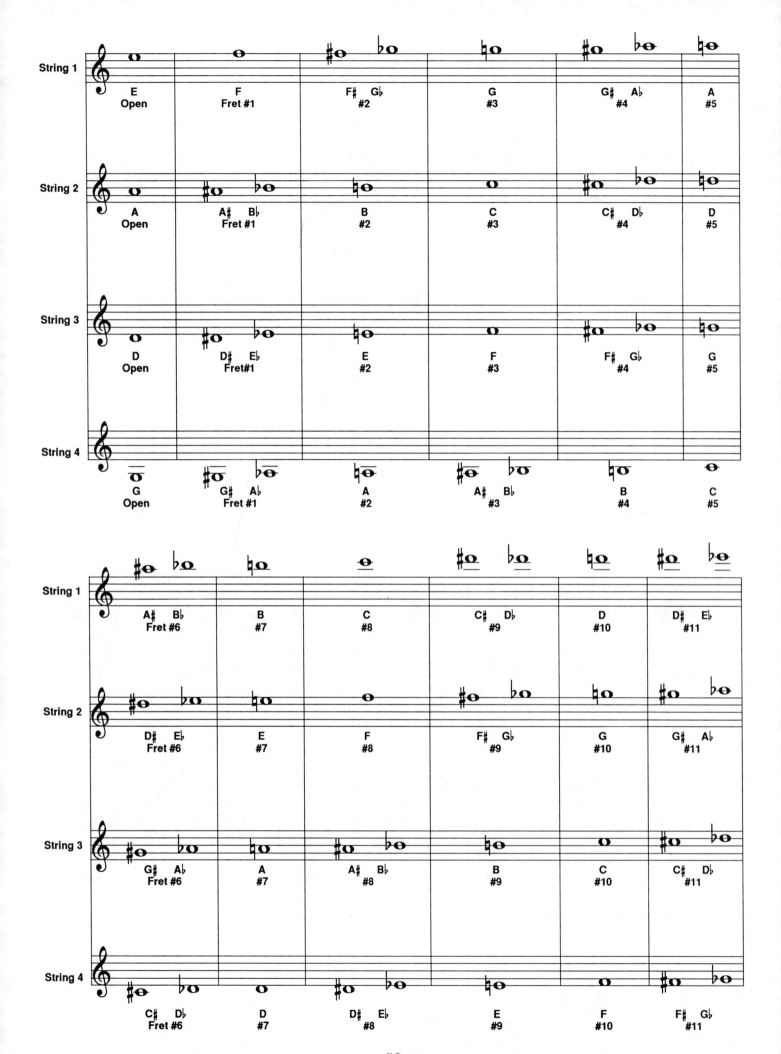

58

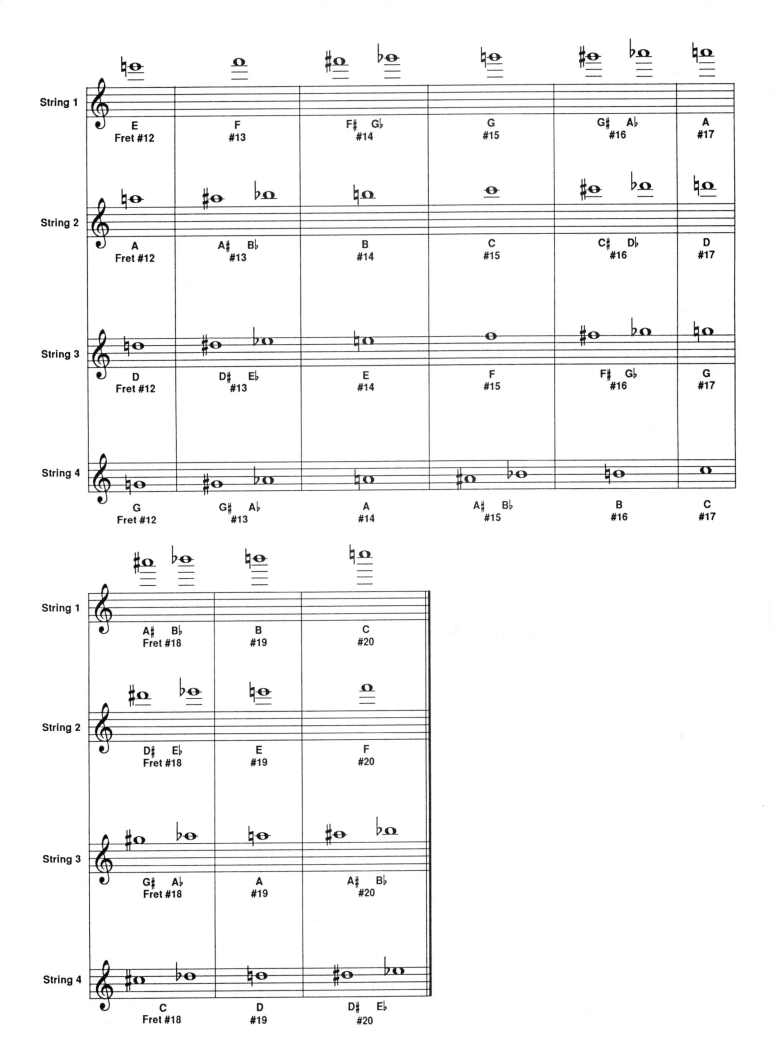

Rhythm

The most common unit of rhythm or time used in this book is the *quarter note:* ♩. We can assign the quarter note any value — one beat, two beats, one-half beat, etc. — and this value is determined by the *time signature* at the beginning of the piece; for example, $\frac{4}{4}$, $\frac{3}{4}$, $\frac{3}{2}$, $\frac{3}{8}$ or $\frac{3}{4}$. You'll remember from our discussion of waltz strums that the top number of the time signature tells how many beats will be in each measure, the bottom number tells which note is equal to one beat. $\frac{3}{8}$ tells us that there are three beats to the measure (top number) and an eighth note gets one beat (bottom number). In $\frac{3}{8}$ a quarter note gets two beats. $\frac{4}{4}$ tells us that there are four beats to the measure (top number) and a quarter note gets one beat (bottom number). All the units of rhythm — whole, half, eighth, sixteenth notes, etc. — no matter what the time signature, are relative to each other and work just like fractions.

1	2	4	8		16
Whole = Note	Half Notes	= Quarter Notes	= Eighth Notes	=	Sixteenth Notes

The bottom number of the time signature defines which kind of note will get one beat; whole, half, eighth, sixteenth, etc. All of the other notes' values are then adjusted accordingly because of their relativity. For example, $\frac{3}{2}$ means three beats to the measure and the half note gets one beat. Adjust the others accordingly and you find that in $\frac{3}{2}$ a whole note gets two beats, a quarter ½ beat, and an eighth ¼ beat.

Eighth, sixteenth, thirty-second, sixty-fourth notes, etc., have flags on their stems (one for eighth, two for sixteenth, etc.). Often you'll see them grouped and tied together for easier reading:

Eighth Notes
Flagged & Grouped

Sixteenth Notes
Flagged & Grouped

If whole, half, and quarter notes are the yin of music, *rests* are the yang. Instead of sound, rests are silences held for the same duration as their sonorous counterparts. Kind of a Northern California, karma kind of koncept.

1	2	4	8		16
Whole Rest	= Half Rests	= Quarter Rests	= Eighth Rests	=	Sixteenth Rests

If you find it difficult to remember which rest is whole, which is half, think of it this way: The half rest looks a little like a hat and the word "hat" sounds a little like the word "half." Hat...Half...Get it? (Not worth calling the *Grove Dictionary of Music* people but it works for me.)

The speed or *tempo* of the music can be as slow as a funeral dirge or as quick as a country fiddle tune. Tempo is determined by the players and is based on the intentions of the composer. No matter what the speed, the relationship between wholes, halves, quarters, etc., remains intact.

Note reading, like riding a bicycle, is a skill that one perfects with practice. It's easy to understand intellectually how to do either; "put your hands here and hold on, put your feet here and pedal," "this space is A, this line is D, this note gets three beats, this note one half beat." It's another thing altogether to be able to stay on the bike and off the pavement or read music off the page, on the job. The more you practice, the easier it will become. Make it part of daily playing routine to read easy unfamiliar music. Don't go over a piece until you memorize it and can play it by ear; that's not the point. What you want to do is train your eye, hands, and brain to translate those spots of ink on the paper directly into music.

Tablature

Tablature is an alternative to music reading. Numbers, which correspond to frets, are arranged on a four-line staff, each line representing one of the strings on the mandolin. Rather than reading notes, the player reads positions. The top line of the tablature staff represents the first string (E) of the mandolin, second from the top is the second string (A), third from the top is the third string (D), and the bottom line is the fourth string (G). (This is the famous "bottom line" that people are always talking about.) The illustration below shows a line of standard notation together with its tablature line.

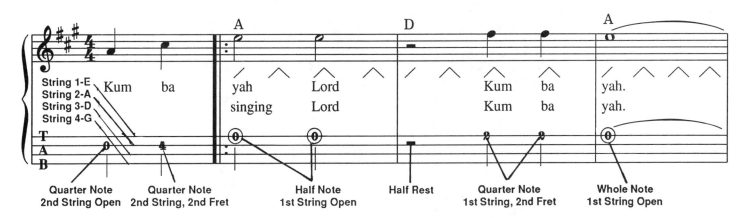

The stems and circles correspond to standard note time values; numbers represent fret numbers.

$$\mathbf{o} = ⑤ \qquad d = ⓪ \qquad \rlap{\raisebox{0.3ex}{\scriptsize|}}d = 2 \qquad \text{♪} = 3 \qquad \text{♪} = 7$$

Rests, slurs, ties, etc., are usually indicated exactly as they are in the standard notation.

While tablature is a valuable tool for beginners it also has serious drawbacks. It's just about as difficult to learn as standard notation, so why not learn the real thing? Also, tablature is not standardized. Sometimes the numbers are on the lines, sometimes on the spaces, sometimes rhythm is indicated, sometimes not. While tablature is almost always included in teaching books like this, it is rarely found in collections of songs or advanced method books. In the short run it works great and lets you play melodies almost immediately. In the long run it's severely limiting. Sooner or later, when you need to read a piece of music that doesn't have tab included, you'll run smack dab into its constraints.

Standard music notation, on the other hand, is universal the world over. Learning even its most basic rudiments opens up your musical world to anything written down, from Bach to The Beatles, show tunes to fiddle tunes, Stephen Foster to Cole Porter, etc., etc. You can communicate with players and composers from every part of the world regardless of language differences. (You can see where my prejudice lies.)

My suggestion is that you use tablature only briefly to orient yourself to the names of the notes on both the printed page and the mandolin fingerboard. Use it to get off to a fast start, to encourage you and reinforce your early progress, but move on to standard notation when it becomes a crutch or roadblock.

Gibson Mandola, H-4, ca. 1915   *Photo by Dix Bruce © 1982*

Stringin'

Pitch is a cut-and-dried concept, "this finger on this fret is an A note," for example. It's even easier if you have tablature. Rhythm is a little more abstract and complicated. You'll find three types of note values in this first simple melody: quarter, half, and whole. Since the piece is in $\frac{4}{4}$ time, quarter notes get one beat, halves two beats, and wholes four beats. When we say that a note "gets" a certain number of beats, we mean that we let it sound for that duration of time.

The numbers below each note in "Stringin'" indicate where the note falls in the four-beat measure. Numbers in parentheses indicate that a note is held over for the duration of this beat and should not be picked separately. Circled numbers above the notes represent fretting-finger numbers, just like in chord diagrams; ① = index, ② = middle, ③ = ring, ④ = pinkie. Don't get these confused with the numbers in the tablature line which indicate fret positions. All the notes are either quarters or halves, so pick them with downstrokes as indicated with this symbol: ↓ .

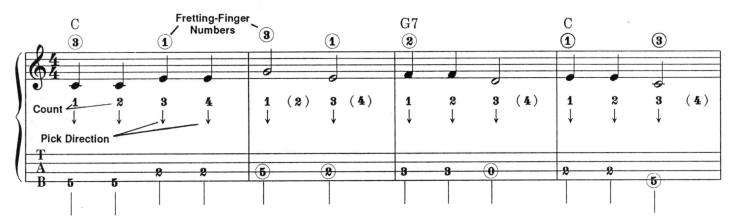

From now on, I'll leave the strum pattern up to you. You can always use the straight-four downstrum or make up your own pattern from those you've already studied. By now you should be able to play the chords you studied in Part I from memory. If you can't, it means you need to review the chords until you have them memorized. To quote Mel Bay, "If not now, when? If not you, who?" (Actually, I don't know if he ever really said that, but I was dying to quote him somewhere in this book.) When you're playing along with the stereo cassette tape, remember that you can use the balance control on your amplifier or tuner to pan to the right or left. This will allow you to hear melody or accompaniment solo so that you can really concentrate on the individual parts.

Remember to use the fingertips of your fretting hand, straight down, to make contact with the strings, just like you've been practicing with chords. (See photo on page 14.) There will be times when you can't avoid a slightly angled approach, but as a rule try to come straight down on the strings with the fingertips.

When picking single notes, many players anchor the fourth finger of their picking hand on the pickguard or top of the mandolin for support. Others let the hand fly free and pivot from their wrist and/or elbow. Still others use an approach somewhere in between. A great controversy rages as to which is best in the long run. I'm in the former camp and find that anchoring the finger gives me strength in my picking hand. I've noticed that it can also limit my reach of the fourth string. Experiment to find what works for you.

Stringin'

Dix Bruce
Key of C

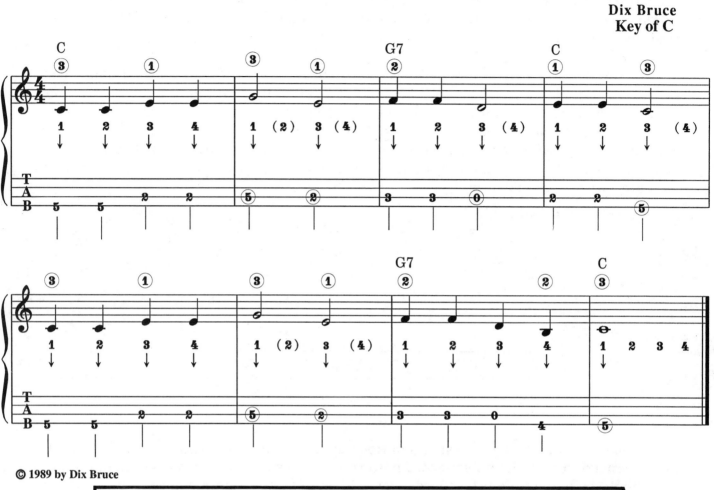

Kentucky KM-1500

Key Signatures

Music can be written and played in any key, A, A♯/B♭, B, C, C♯/D♭, D, D♯/E♭, E, F, F♯/G♭, G, or G♯/A♭. Each key has its own distinct major scale (do-re-me-fa-so-la-ti-do) with set intervals between its eight notes: 1-(whole step-two frets)-2-(whole step)-3-(half step-one fret)-4-(whole step)-5-(whole step)-6-(whole step)-7-(half step)-8. Every major scale, no matter which note it begins on, preserves this "whole, whole, half, whole, whole, whole, half" set of intervals. The diagram below illustrates this.

1		2		3		4		5		6		7		8
C	∨	D	∨	E	∨	F	∨	G	∨	A	∨	B	∨	C
	whole step		whole step		half step		whole step		whole step		whole step		half step	

"Stringin'" is written in the key of C using notes from the C major scale C, D, E, F, G, A, B, C. The next song, "The No-Name Rag," is written in the key of G using notes from the G major scale G, A, B, C, D, E, F♯, G. In order to preserve the required major scale whole step–half step interval pattern, we have to raise the F note one half step to F♯. This is reflected in the tune's *key signature* where we add a ♯ (*sharp*) sign to the top or F line of the staff. Adding the sharp in the key signature changes all the F notes in the piece to F♯ notes.

One sharp sign in the key signature will always mean that the piece is written in the key of G. Each key and major scale have a different key signature, up to seven sharps or flats. Keys with sharps in the key signature are commonly referred to as *sharp keys;* keys with flats in the key signature are called (what else?) *flat keys.* The key of C, which has no sharps or flats, sits the fence between sharp and flat keys. It is included as a reference in both of the following diagrams.

Sharp keys:

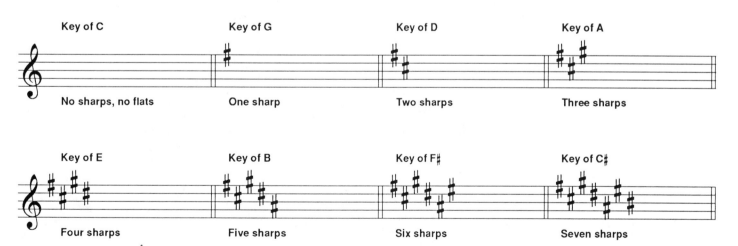

65

Flat keys:

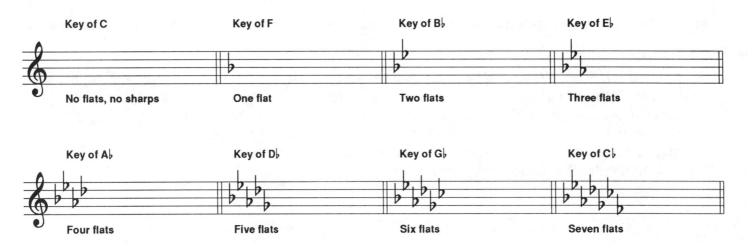

How will you ever remember all that? Easy — we cut corners by remembering two rules and memorizing a couple of exceptions. If the key signature has no sharps or flats, the piece is in the key of C. C is a special case that doesn't fit in with the following rules.

Rule 1: To determine the key name of a piece with sharps in the key signature, find the sharp sign furthest to the right in the key signature. Then simply read up one half step on the staff — that's your key. Let's try it with the key of G. The only sharp sign is on the F line, making it F♯. Go up one half step from F♯ to G, and *shazam,* key of G. What's the name of the key with five sharps? The furthest sharp sign to the right is on the A space, making it A♯. Up one half step and we're at B, so five sharps tells us the piece is in the key of B. Arithmetic and show biz, what a team!

Figuring flat keys is just as easy. **Rule 2:** Find the flat sign *second* from the right in the key signature. Whatever line or space it's on names the key. Try it with three flats. The second flat from the right is on the E space, making it E♭, and thus the key of E♭. There's one exception, and this is the other thing you have to memorize. Since the key of F has only one flat (B♭) in its key signature, you can't look to its left to figure the key. So, just remember that one flat always means the key of F. After that the regular rule applies.

Major Scales

It's important to be familiar with the scales that are implied by the different key signatures. All are shown below in abbreviated form within easy reach at the bottom of the neck. Some have open-string notes, others are in closed, moveable positions. Most can be extended up and down the neck or transposed to other keys. More on that in a minute. You'll find that certain keys are more common than others. Chances are you won't see a lot of mandolin music written in more than four or five sharps or flats. Learn the scales with a few sharps or flats before you tackle the others. Work through them gradually, one or two a day, playing them slowly as warm-up exercises. Play them first as all downstrokes, then alternate up and down strokes. It won't hurt to learn them in several positions.

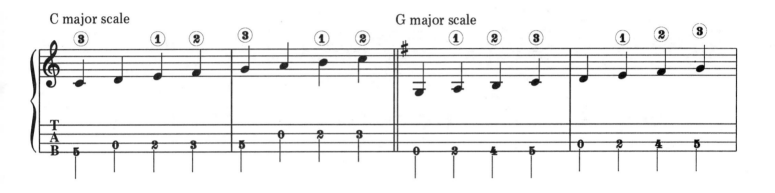

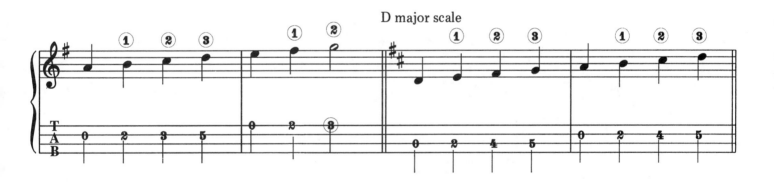

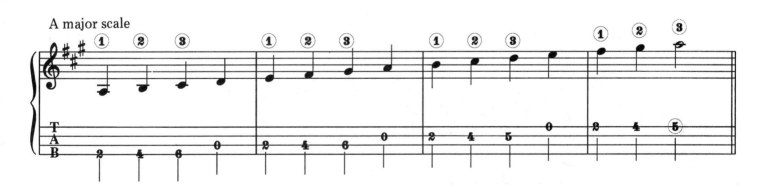

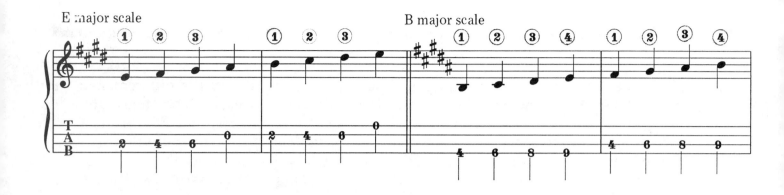

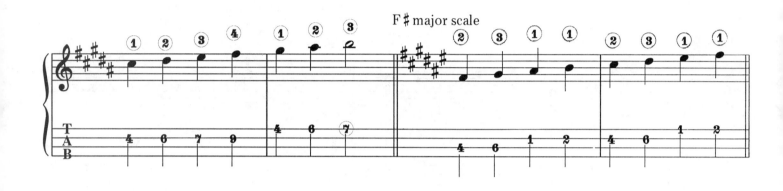

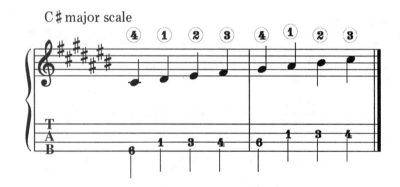

Major Scales for Flat Keys

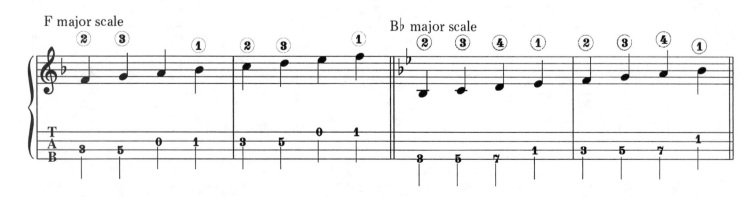

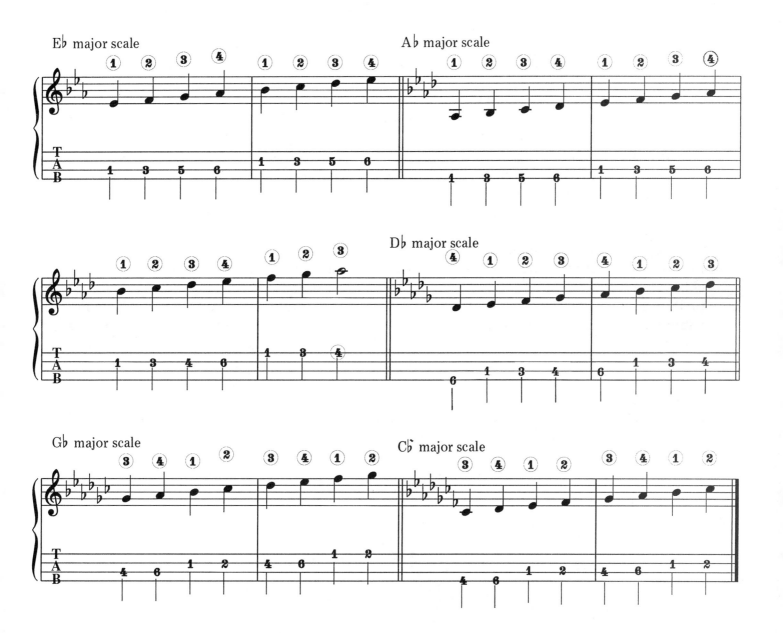

By now you know that one of the major themes of this book is recycling. "Cash for my trash?" you ask. Not exactly. (You already do that with your bottles, cans, and newspapers, don't you? Good for you!) This type of recycling involves learning one thing and using it in several new and different applications. For example, a closed-position chord (one that has no open strings) can be moved intact to make many new chords. With that in mind, let's look again at the scales above and try to recycle them. (Wait until you've got a pretty good handle on the scales as written before you try this exercise.)

The C major scale has open-string notes, so it isn't movable up or down the neck like a closed-position scale. Still we can get a little more mileage out of it. What would happen if we moved this basic C major scale position over one string and started it on the third string, fifth fret rather than the fourth string? (Different notes, same position.) Right, we get a G major scale which looks suspiciously like the latter half of the G scale shown. Now move the G major scale shown over one string and begin on the open D string. Play it as far up as you dare on the first string. OK, you're way ahead of me. Presto! The D scale.

Now move the D major scale shown over one string so that it begins on the open A string. Again you'll find that it looks like the second half of the A scale which follows. Move the A major scale shown over one string so that it begins on the third string, second fret. Whoopie! The E scale.

69

The B major scale is your first closed-position scale and has no open-string notes. Not only can you move closed-position scales from string to string, you can also move them up and down the neck. Try shifting the B major up one fret and begin on the fourth string, fifth fret. This gives you the C major scale. Move this scale back down two frets and you get the Bb. I could go on and on, but that's for you to do. The point of all of this is to show you how to use one position in a variety of ways. You're also learning how closely interrelated all the scales and keys are. To continue this work, try moving all the flat scales vertically and horizontally. Extend all the scales with open-string notes as far up the neck as you can. Finally, if you're really ambitious, pick any note on the neck and construct separate major-scale positions starting with each of your four fretting-hand fingers. The trick is to not move your hand too much.

Keys are sometimes named by their *relative minor* chord. The relative minor is built on the sixth note of the major scale. In the key of C the relative minor is Am; the relative minor of F is Dm. If the chords and melody center around this minor sound, the key may be referred to as "A minor" or "D minor," though the key signature remains the same as for the major equivalent. As an exercise, look at the scales above and determine the sixth or relative minor of each key.

If you look back at the songs you learned in Part I, you'll notice a variety of keys. Notice also that each key has a different set of chords that go along with it. In addition to major scales, each key has minor and modal scales. If you study music theory you'll discover how all these chords, keys, and scales interrelate.

Gibson F-5 Lloyd Loar

70

The No-Name Rag

"The No-Name Rag" will be a small step for some, a giant leap for others of you out there in the vast mandolin world. It introduces several new concepts about written music and playing, including eighth notes. If you are among those who find it particularly challenging, give it time, start slow, be patient. Work up to playing along with the tape by reviewing "Kumbaya," "Streets of Laredo," "Careless Love," "I Ride an Old Paint," and trying to play their relatively simple quarter-note melodies. Keep in mind that it *can* be done and that *you* can do it!

The first unusual thing you'll notice about "The No-Name Rag" is a **C** where you'd expect the time signature to be. Does this mean that the tune is in the key of C? Not on your life! **C** is an abbreviation for *common time*, which is another term for $\frac{4}{4}$, so **C** = $\frac{4}{4}$.

"No-Name" begins with a *pickup*. A pickup is (among other things) an incomplete measure at the beginning of a piece. It works like an introduction. In this tune the pickup has only three beats and is counted "Two, three, four" as shown, without beat one.

A pickup may or may not be included in a repeat. In this tune it's not repeated because it's integrated into the first ending. By the way, throughout this book I've often called your attention to a specific measure in a piece by referring to it as the fourth "full" measure or the first "complete" measure. Obviously if you're counting into a piece from the beginning, you'll skip the pickup, which is neither full nor complete since it has fewer beats than defined by the time signature.

The first complete measure has eight eighth notes. Since two eighth notes equal one quarter note and a quarter note is held for one beat, each eighth note is held for one half beat. We count eighth notes as follows:

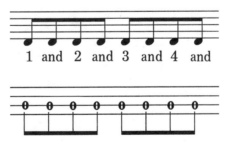

If you're a foot tapper you'll need to mentally subdivide your tap into an up and a down stroke. Keep your tap speed exactly the same, but think "One, two, three, four" as your foot hits the floor, "and" as it hits the uppermost point of its upstroke. See the following diagram.

Count...	ONE	AND	TWO	AND	THREE	AND	FOUR	AND
Foot	down	up	down	up	down	up	down	up

By the way, "ands" are noted in the music copy as pluses (+).

Now that we're playing eighth notes we need to be concerned about pick direction. Downstrokes just won't get the job done efficiently any more, we'll need to add in upstrokes. My rule is this: **If the note begins on beat one, two, three, or four, play it with a downstroke (noted in music with this symbol: ↓). If it begins on one of the "ands" between the beats, play it with an upstroke (↑).** It doesn't matter if the note is an eighth, quarter, half, or whole. Here are some notated examples.

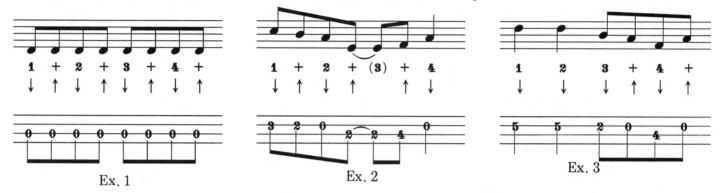

Ex. 1   Ex. 2   Ex. 3

Pick direction should also be coordinated with your foot tapping; pick a downstroke when the note begins on a foot downstroke, upstroke when the note begins on a foot upstroke. By the way, notation for pick direction is by no means uniform. I use arrows since they seem most logical. The classical mando-mavens differ in their use of symbols: Bickford says ⊓ = down, V = up; Christofaro and Pettine agree that ∧ = down, ⊔ = up; and Hladky uses ∧ = down, V = up. The Bickford approach is borrowed from violin notation; the down symbol (⊓) is supposed to remind you to move in the direction of the frog of the bow, the up symbol (V) is supposed to remind you to move in the direction of the tip (or toad) of the bow. If you're reading a Bach violin sonata, that's probably what you'll see.

For right now, consider this rule carved in stone. After you've mastered the basics you may discover that certain difficult passages can be played easier or smoother by deviating from the pick direction rule.

In the seventh measure, two eighth notes are connected with a *tie*.

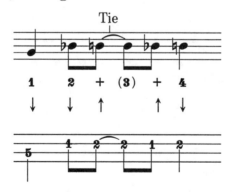

When two or more notes are tied, the pitch is held for the duration of the notes enclosed by the tie, though only the first note is picked. In this case you'll pick two upstrokes in a row. Listen to the taped example of the tie. The pick patterns shown in the first few measures should be extrapolated throughout the piece. Stick to the rule and soon you won't have to think about direction at all; it'll become second nature.

Also in the seventh measure you'll see the notation "G (Chord tacit—)." Strum the G chord on beat one of measure seven and leave it out altogether for the duration of the *tacit* (through measure eight), even though the melody continues. A tacit works like a rest for chords. Play it two different ways: Let it ring after beat one, or damp the sound.

Finally, you'll see endings noted like this:

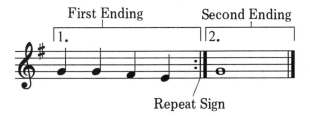

When you reach the repeat sign in the first ending :‖ , go back to the beginning of the piece and continue from the reverse repeat sign: ‖: . Repeat signs are usually used in pairs like this ‖: :‖ and indicate that whatever is enclosed within them should be repeated. Since the first measure pickup is not enclosed, you shouldn't repeat it. If there is no reverse repeat near the beginning of the piece, repeat from the first note. When you get back down to the first ending, skip it and continue to the second ending, which ends the piece.

The "Best Laid Plans of Mice & Men" Mandolin   *Photo by Dix Bruce © 1982*

The No-Name Rag

Key of G

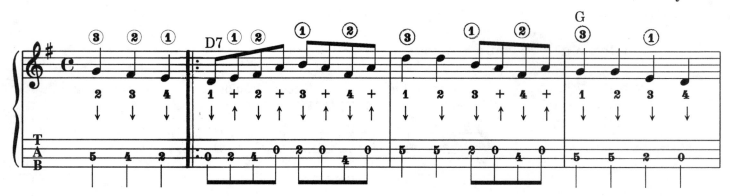

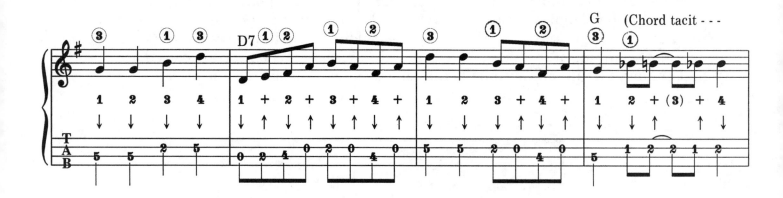

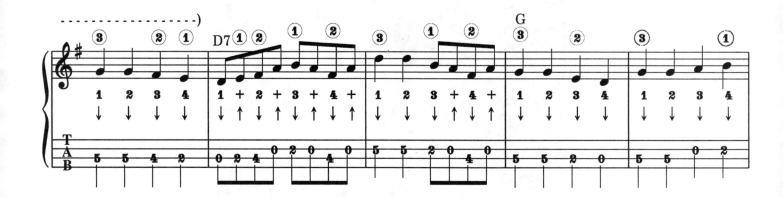

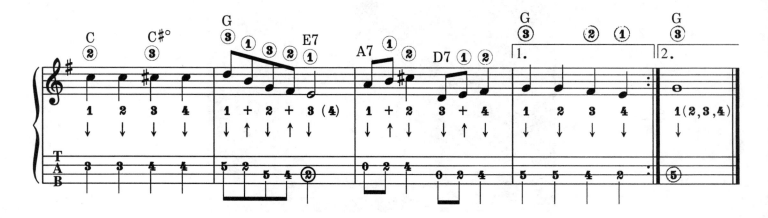

74

As I mentioned earlier, the symmetrical nature of the mandolin allows you to move chords and melodies around easily. Since all of the notes in "No-Name" fall on strings two and three, you can move this melody to the other string pairs — one and two or three and four — by simply shifting over one string. Keep in mind that a move of this type will change the key and accompanying chords along with the melody, just as in the scale exercise you did on page 69.

The original version of "No-Name" is in the key of G and begins on a G note (third string, fifth fret). Try starting it on the fourth-string, fifth-fret C instead. Maintain the same basic hand position as the G version. Don't think too much about the names of the notes you're playing; concentrate on position.

Any guess as to what the new key is? Try a little deductive reasoning. If the first note of the key-of-G version is a G note and the first note of our new version is a C note, then our new version must be in the key of . . . C, right? Once you get the hang of the new key, play along with the taped version. You won't find it written out because I want this to be a mental exercise.

Well, if we can move the melody across the strings in one direction, why not try the other? Refresh your memory of the key-of-G version. Now move everything over so that your first note is a D (second string, fifth fret). You already know what key it's going to be in, don't you? Practice with the tape. Now you can play "No-Name" in three keys: G, C, and D. You're practically ready for MTV or even *The Tonight Show!* Experiment with moving other melodies, and in the process you'll unlock the secrets of playing in any key on the mandolin.

The Washburn 4-String Electric

Swing Low, Sweet Chariot

Notes with dots after them are called (this is beautiful) *dotted notes*. Here's a *dotted half note* ♩. and a *dotted quarter note* ♩. . A dot after a note adds one half of the note's value to the note. It works like a good union, stretching the note to time and a half. In $\frac{4}{4}$ a half note gets two beats, so a dotted half note gets three beats (2 plus 1 — ½ of 2 — equals 3). In $\frac{4}{4}$ a quarter note gets one beat, so a dotted quarter gets one and one half beats. A whole note gets four beats, so a dotted whole gets six. Dots can also be applied to rests.

If you're like everyone else, myself included, you'll find it difficult at first to count dotted notes, especially dotted quarter notes. One way to learn and remember these rhythms is to relate them to a lyric in a well known song. The chorus to "Swing Low" has both dotted halves and quarters. Sing the word "chariot" and you'll get a pretty good idea how to play the dotted quarter note.

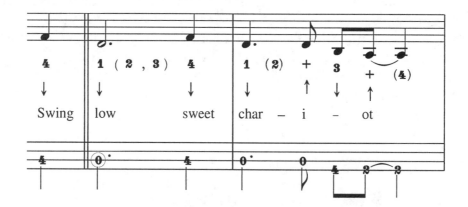

As is often the case, the dotted half is followed by a quarter, the dotted quarter by an eighth. Be sure to include these following notes as you practice dotted note rhythms. It's often difficult to get a correct feel if you isolate the notes from their neighbors. Speak the lyrics as you tap your foot and listen to the taped examples. Pay close attention to the pick direction markings.

Written music, especially very complex classical music, does a good job of describing how a given piece should sound. Even so, anything written down is open to your interpretation as a player. These songs are written very simply with rather straight rhythms for ease of understanding. You've probably heard "Swing Low Sweet Chariot" performed in a number of ways from shouting gospel to low-down blues. You can play it any way you feel. Once you know the notes, put your own personality into it and feel free to jazz it up or punch the rhythm. Don't feel bound by what's on the page or the tape. Make it your own!

Swing Low, Sweet Chariot

Sally Goodin

Since the mandolin and violin are tuned exactly the same, much of the repertoire of one is playable on the other. Mandolinists can adapt a whole range of violin music from classical to jazz to country. "Sally Goodin" is an old-time fiddle tune.

You'll notice two new notations in the music, *ho* for hammer-on (measure one) and *po* for pull-off (measure two). Both are fretting-hand maneuvers that allow you to play two notes on the same string with only one pick stroke. Hammers work from a lower to a higher note; pulls from a higher to a lower note. Both are indicated in standard notation with *slur* markings. Slurs look just like ties except that they connect two different pitches while ties connect two notes of the same pitch.

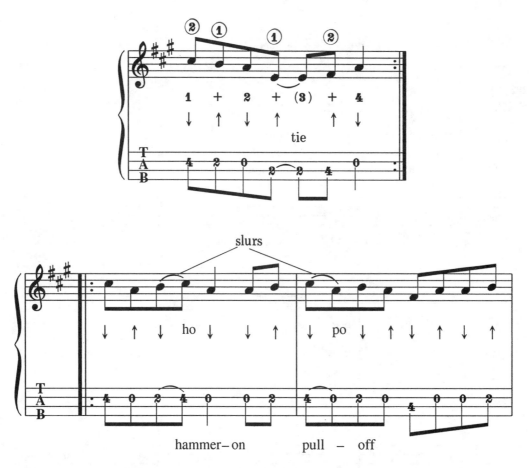

To play the hammer in measure one, first pick the B note (second string, second fret), and while the B is still ringing quickly fret the C♯ (second string, fourth fret) with your second finger. The C♯ should ring even though you haven't picked it.

To play the pull-off in measure two, pick the C♯ (second string, fourth fret) with your second finger and, while it's still ringing, push the second finger off and let the open string ring.

Sally Goodin

You can also play hammer-on or pull-off slurs with *slides* where you slide your fretting finger up or down to the next note or notes. Substitute slides for all the hammers and pulls in "Sally Goodin." Below you'll find the first line. Notice that some of the finger changes, e.g., the fourth note of the first full measure, have been removed since a slide involves sliding with one finger to play two or more notes.

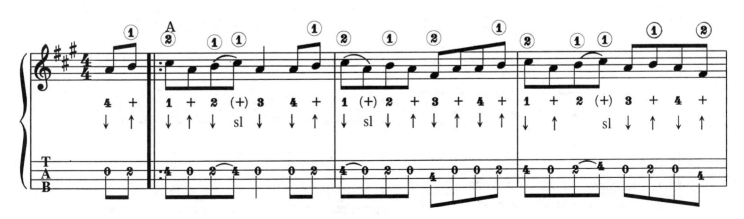

79

Fair & Tender Ladies

In all the years I've played mandolin, the *only* fault I can find with the instrument is that it doesn't have much sustain. You pick a note and it quickly dies away. Luckily there's a solution. With a technique called *tremolo* you can sustain a note all day, all night, and on into next week. Fiddlers have bowing, we have tremolo!

At its best, tremolo is a smooth, seamless, continuous up-and-down picking of the strings that sounds like one sustained note. It allows the mandolinist to play beautiful legato passages and is a wonderful dynamic tool when played at different speeds and intensities. David Grisman is the king of the beautiful tremolo and has a right hand that just won't quit. Listen to how his brilliant use of tremolo infuses his playing with soul and emotion.

In essence the tremolo technique breaks a long note down into several shorter notes played with down and up strokes. For example, you'd normally use one downstroke to play a quarter-note G. To tremolo the same note, you might play it as though it were four sixteenth notes. To play a faster tremolo you might think of that same quarter note as eight thirty-second notes. Obviously the more notes you try to squeeze in, the more challenging it will be.

Like any other skill worth a hoot, it takes some practice to master. Look at the open-string whole notes below.

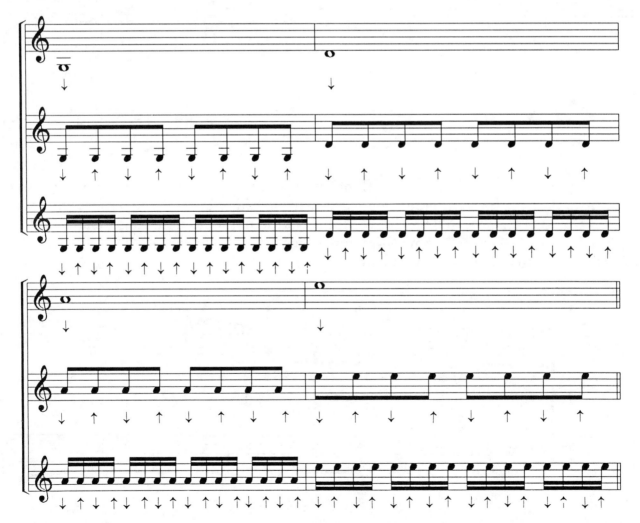

First play them slowly as you normally would with single downstrokes, taking special care to hold each one out to its full four counts. Next play each whole note as though it were eight eighth notes. Gradually increase the speed of your picking until the notes form one continuous sound without stops and starts. This will probably take months to smooth out.

Practice tremolo on all note values — eighth, quarter, half, etc. Tremolo all the major scales. Tremolo in the tub, during meals, etc. Build up those picking-hand muscles. Experiment with a faster tremolo by substituting sixteen sixteenth notes for each whole. There's no one perfect tremolo or standard tremolo speed. To strengthen your tremolo, play it continuously through melodies. As you'll discover, different speeds give different effects. Be sure to listen to the taped examples.

"Fair and Tender Ladies" sounds best when you use tremolo on the longer notes, like dotted halves and wholes. Be sure to play through all of the verses for added practice. Review the other tunes you've learned and play their melodies with tremolo, especially the longer notes. (Incidentally, tremolo is sometimes noted in sheet music like this ♪ ♩. . Unfortunately this symbol sometimes means to arpeggiate a chord, so I don't use it.)

There are no firm rules on when to tremolo unless a composer specifically notates tremolo in a piece. It's a tool you can use anywhere you need a sustained note. Practice tremolo on slow tunes and long notes.

You'll notice that the counting numbers and pick direction markings under the notes have disappeared; you're on your own! If you're still a little shaky on the subject, review the rules and then pencil in pick direction arrows throughout "Fair and Tender Ladies." Here's an annotated excerpt to get you started. Most of the tune follows this outline.

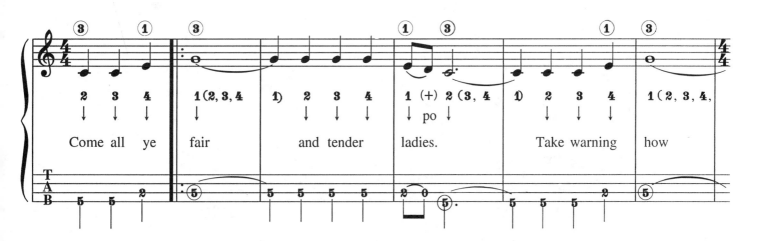

Fair and Tender Ladies

Key of C

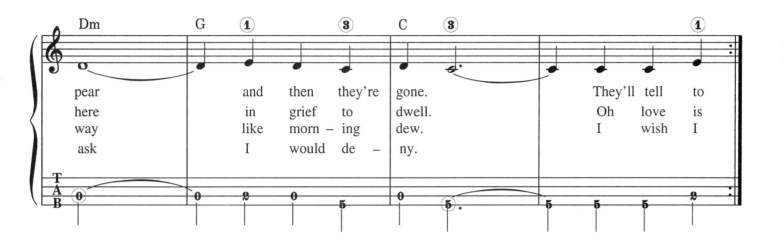

pear   and   then   they're   gone.   They'll   tell   to
here   in   grief   to   dwell.   Oh   love   is
way   like   morn – ing   dew.   I   wish   I
ask   I   would   de – ny.

Roberts "Tiny Moore" 5-String Electric

All Through the Night

Up to now you've been playing chords or single notes on the mandolin. You can also play *double stops,* two notes at a time, to harmonize melody lines. This arrangement of "All Through the Night" demonstrates double stops and how they work.

Here's part of the melody to "All Through the Night."

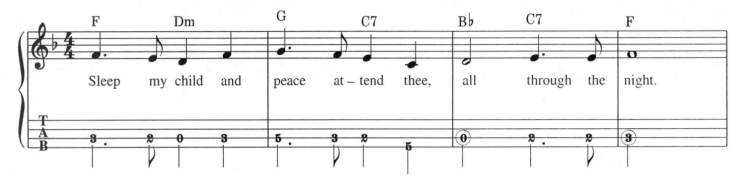

Here's a simple harmony to the melody above.

Now here are both parts combined:

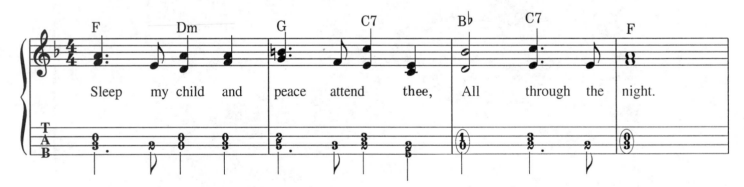

Learn the melody first by playing only the lower notes. When you move on to the double-stop version, follow the fingering directions carefully. You can also play this tune as a duet with a musical buddy. One of you plays the upper notes, one the lower. When there's only one note shown, like the E note in the second measure, you should both play it.

Though it looks like a lot to learn, don't panic! On closer examination you'll see that the melody is quite repetitious. The second four bars are a repeat of the first four. The third four are new, but the last four are a repeat of the first four again. You really have to learn only eight bars of material for a sixteen-bar piece. Such a deal, you're coming out way ahead of the game. In a nutshell that's why I'm in the music business!

The following is an excerpt marked with pick directions and counting numbers. For an added challenge, work on tremolo double stops. WARNING: You still have to play the pitches and rhythms clearly.

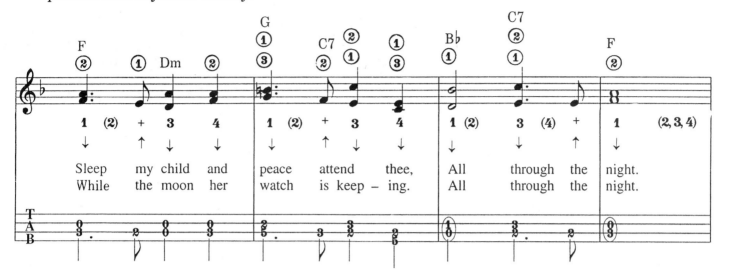

Fun with the Mandolin   *Photo by Dix Bruce © Copyright 1990*

All Through the Night

Sleep my child and peace attend thee, All through the night.
While the moon her watch is keep – ing. All through the night.

Guardian an – gels God will send thee, All through the night.
While the wea – ry world is sleep – ing All through the night.

Soft the drow – sy hours are creeping, Hill and vale in slumber sleeping.
O'er thy spir – it gent – ly steal – ing, Visions of de – light re – vealing.

I my lov – ing vig – il keeping. All through the night.
breathes a pure and ho – ly feeling. All through the night.

Both the techniques of tremolo and double stops are very important to the well-rounded intermediate player. What I've demonstrated so far is only an introduction to each. For further study listen to the great players listed in the back of this book and consult more advanced texts.

Dix Bruce: The more he plays mandolin, the younger he looks! This can work for you, too!
Photo by Harry Orner

Beginning at the End

Congratulations! You've made it through! Take a deep breath, give your mandolin a pat on the back, and shake your own hand. That done, it's now time to go back to the songs in the first part of this book and try playing their melodies. (We don't waste a minute!)

Each song includes a boxed annotated excerpt. In it you'll find specific playing tips, counting and pick direction clues, and fretting-finger information. I didn't annotate the entire pieces for several reasons. The extra information takes up a lot of room. Including it all makes it difficult to see individual components, especially for beginners who need to see only the lyrics and strum patterns. You'll also find that most of the finger, counting, and pick direction patterns repeat throughout the piece. Once you've looked the excerpt over, you can extrapolate the information to the rest of the song, especially if you follow the basic rules of counting and pick direction. This will help you develop your note-reading skills on the mandolin.

In some cases your attention will be directed to a specific measure number, for example, "the ninth full measure." Remember, when the term "full measure" is used, start counting *after* the pickup with the first complete measure.

Practice your tremolo on every song, especially those with notes longer than quarters. Don't be afraid to improvise your own melodies with added notes, hammers, pulls, and slides. Some of the songs will be more challenging than others, though all should be within easy reach of anyone who's come this far. Before you try playing them, review each song's key signature and practice the applicable scale (page 67). Play along with the tape; I'll be waiting to pick with you!

Don't forget to listen to mandolin live and on record. Several of my favorite mandolin records are listed in the sources section. As you listen, try to play what you hear by ear. Start by figuring out chord progressions to simple tunes. Then try simple melodies and easy solos. You may find it helpful to listen to song excerpts at ½ speed by utilizing a two-speed tape recorder. Eventually this process will train your ears, brain, and hands to work together. The ultimate goal is to be able to play anything you hear. You won't have to rely on sheet music! Community colleges often offer courses in *ear training* where the student learns to identify and sing all of the intervals and chords. There are also a few commercially available taped ear-training courses on the market.

I've enjoyed working on this book and hope you've enjoyed my efforts. Write to me with your comments, questions, or jokes c/o Musix, P.O. Box 231005, Pleasant Hill, CA 94523.

Scale, Chord, and Transposition Chart

    The chart on the following page can be used to determine major scales for all the keys, key signatures, chords in major keys, and as a transposition guide. Each key is shown with its major scale and identified by the number of accidentals (sharps or flats) it contains. (See the "♯/♭" column.) With this information you can look at any key signature and determine the key. Scales are listed horizontally with Arabic numerals, chords with Roman numerals. To read a scale simply ignore the chord markings (*m* for minor or ° for diminished). To determine chords, read horizontally as shown. For example, the scale for the key of B♭ (two flats) is:

B♭	C	D	E♭	F	G	A	B♭
1	2	3	4	5	6	7	8

The chords for the same key are:

B♭	Cm	Dm	E♭	F	Gm	A°	B♭
I	ii	iii	IV	V	vi	vii°	VIII

    This information can help you transpose from one key to another. Here's how: Let's say you know a tune in the key of D but want to be able to play it in the key of G where it's best for your voice. Unfortunately you don't know what chords to play in the new key of G. The key-of-D chords, which you already know, are D, G, and A. From the chart you can see that the D is the I chord, the G is the IV, and the A is the V. To transpose these chords to the key of G, just follow down in their respective columns (I, ii, iii, etc.) to the new key. This will tell you to substitute Gs for all the D chords, Cs for all the G chords, and Ds for all the A chords. Like numbers are always substituted — I to I, ii to ii, vii° to vii°, etc.

    You can also transpose note by note with the chart. Continuing with the above example, let's say the first note of the tune in the key of D is an F♯ and you need to know what the first note in the key of G will be. Find the key-of-D line in the chart, read over horizontally until you come to the F♯, which happens to be in the "3" column. Stay in the "3" column and follow down to the key-of-G line — *presto* — you see that the first note of our tune in the key of G is B.

Key	♯/♭		Scale	1	2	3	4	5	6	7	8
			Chord	I	ii	iii	IV	V	vi	vii°	VIII
C	none			C	Dm	Em	F	G	Am	B°	C
F	1♭			F	Gm	Am	B♭	C	Dm	E°	F
B♭	2♭			B♭	Cm	Dm	E♭	F	Gm	A°	B♭
E♭	3♭			E♭	Fm	Gm	A♭	B♭	Cm	D°	E♭
A♭	4♭			A♭	B♭m	Cm	D♭	E♭	Fm	G°	A♭
D♭	5♭			D♭	E♭m	Fm	G♭	A♭	B♭	C°	D♭
G♭	6♭			G♭	A♭m	B♭m	C♭	D♭	E♭	F°	G♭
C♭	7♭			C♭	D♭m	E♭m	F♭	G♭	A♭m	B♭°	C♭
C♯	7♯			C♯	D♯m	E♯m	F♯	G♯	A♯m	B♯°	C♯
F♯	6♯			F♯	G♯m	A♯m	B	C♯	D♯m	E♯°	F♯
B	5♯			B	C♯m	D♯m	E	F♯	G♯m	A♯°	B
E	4♯			E	F♯m	G♯m	A	B	C♯m	D♯°	E
A	3♯			A	Bm	C♯m	D	E	F♯m	G♯°	A
D	2♯			D	Em	F♯m	G	A	Bm	C♯°	D
G	1♯			G	Am	Bm	C	D	Em	F♯°	G

Numbers

90